The Little Book of
Computer Wisdom

Books by Charles Rubin

Thinking Small: The Buyer's Guide to Portable Computers
The Endless Apple
AppleWorks: Boosting Your Business with Integrated Software
Command Performance: AppleWorks
Microsoft Works on the Apple Macintosh
Macintosh Hard Disk Management
Running Microsoft Works
The Macintosh Bible "What Do I Do Now?" Book
The Macintosh Bible Guide to System 7
The Macintosh Bible Guide to FileMaker Pro
The Macintosh Bible Guide to System 7.1
The Macintosh Bible Guide to ClarisWorks 2.0
The Little Book of Computer Wisdom

The Little Book of Computer Wisdom

HOW TO MAKE FRIENDS WITH YOUR PC OR MAC

CHARLES RUBIN

Houghton Mifflin Company

Boston   New York

For information about permission to reproduce selections from
this book, write to Permissions, Houghton Mifflin Company,
215 Park Avenue South, New York, New York 10003.

Library of Congress Cataloging-in-Publication Data
Rubin, Charles, date.
    The little book of computer wisdom : how to make friends
with your PC or Mac / Charles Rubin.
        p.   cm.
    Includes index.
    ISBN 0-395-70816-8 (pbk)
    1. Microcomputers. 2. Macintosh (Computer).   I. Title.
QA76.5.R74 1995   94-23188
004.16 — dc 20   CIP

Printed in the United States of America

BP 10 9 8 7 6 5 4 3 2

Book design by Melodie Wertelet

For Sara

Acknowledgments

My deepest thanks go to Claudette Moore, my agent and friend, for encouraging me to write this book, for helping to shape its contents, and for not giving up. I'm also grateful to Harry Foster at Houghton Mifflin Company for his enthusiasm about this project, for his careful review of the manuscript, and for his many helpful suggestions. Thanks to you both for sharing your wisdom with me.

Contents

Introduction

Personal computers are really amazing. Never before have so many of us been so confused and intimidated by something that can be so useful. Never before has one product meant so many different things to so many different people. Never before have so many tried to understand something so difficult.

If personal computers were like any other product, we would all be pretty well up to speed on them by now. After all, they've been around for about twenty years, which should be plenty of time to learn how to push a few buttons and get a clear mental picture of just what they are and what they do.

But a personal computer isn't like any other product. It takes a long time to understand how a computer really operates and to reach a comfort zone that allows you to get it to do what you want.

One way to reach this comfort zone is to spend years working with different computers and programs, as I have. After a while, experience teaches you what all computers and programs have in common, so you get a handle on what they can and can't do.

If you're pressed for time, though, this book can help you become more comfortable more quickly. It offers tidbits of wisdom that can bring you in weeks to the comfort zone I spent years reaching, which many people never reach at all. And believe me, that comfort zone is a place worth reaching.

Ignorance Is Expensive

When you don't understand computers, buying one is a crap-shoot and using one is like walking a tightrope. You push this key and that, sticking closely to a particular set of tasks you've learned and hoping you don't make a mistake and blow the thing up. You learn just enough to get by with the computer, but not enough to enjoy using it. When an unfamiliar screen appears or something unusual happens, you panic.

When you do understand a computer, it becomes invisible. You're able to see the work, game, or information beyond the keys and buttons. You know the limits of what the computer can do, what can and can't happen and why. You can focus on the computing job at hand rather than on the computer you're using to do it. You can solve common problems quickly and without panicking.

The computing comfort zone isn't just an IBM PC comfort zone or a WordPerfect comfort zone or a Mac comfort zone, either. It's a basic understanding that transcends any particular computer or program. It allows you to walk up to any computer and figure out how to turn it on, run a program, and work that program without having seen it before.

Although there are more than 150 million personal computers in the world, some persistent myths about them still prevent people from even beginning to understand them and from finding a proper role for them in their lives. Before we see precisely how this book can transport you to the computer comfort zone, let's clear up these misconceptions.

Computers Really Are Different

Computers aren't like anything else you've ever used. People who sell computers would have you believe that they are just glorified typewriters with televisions on top, but there's a lot more to them than that.

When it comes to scientific or technological discoveries, computers are right up there with electricity and movable type as a transforming force in our lives. Once somebody figured out that any kind of information could be stored and manipulated on a computer, the jobs these machines could perform became nearly unlimited.

Computers can tell time, play music, read books, alter photographs or video images, run machinery, and store, play back, and reproduce written words or numbers, sounds, and pictures. But such versatility is also part of what makes them so difficult to understand.

A computer can behave like lots of familiar devices (a typewriter, a calculator, or a sketchpad, for example), but it isn't just like any of them. A button on the microwave or TV does only one thing. But when you press a key on a computer, you might start a program, erase a sentence, play a sound, or do any of a hundred other things.

Computers are more complicated than most other products we use every day. Every electronic product is technically complex, but most of them keep the complexity on the inside so we don't have to worry about it. On a microwave or stereo or TV, all that complexity is reduced to a few simple buttons or knobs. On a computer, the complexity is right at the surface. We have to learn new ways of working, such as inserting diskettes, pressing several keys at once, and pointing to pictures on a video screen. And as we try to learn how to work with computers, we come upon lots of new words. Even familiar words like *file, memory, mouse, document,* and *button* have new meanings in the world of computing.

Computers also make us think in the abstract. What we see on the computer screen is only part of what's going on. We can store information on a disk, but we don't actually see how or where it's stored. Millions of instructions are flying around inside the computer every second, and it's difficult to visualize just what's going on and to understand why we don't get the results we expect.

Computers are different, all right. But different isn't necessarily bad. It's just a barrier to understanding, like the barriers that often separate people of different cultures. As you gain experience with your computer, you'll cross that barrier and discover just how useful and friendly it can be.

Computing Is Not Programming

Computers don't do anything without a program, a recorded set of instructions that tells them what to do. Whenever you use a computer, you're using a program. But using a program and writing a program are two entirely different things.

In the early days of personal computing, few programs were available, so anyone using a computer had to write his or her own to make the machine do different things. But these days, you'll find off-the-shelf programs for just about anything you could want to do with a computer. The only people who need to learn programming now are professional programmers and serious hobbyists.

Everyone who uses computers uses programs, but you don't need to know how to write one to enter the comfort zone.

The Computer Is Not in Charge

Although it often seems like it, computers aren't in charge of anything. They are so versatile and they process information so quickly that it can sometimes seem as if they're taking control of our lives. But everything on a computer happens because someone makes it happen. Human beings write and operate the programs, and the programs are what make the computer do things. The computer is just following orders.

Sometimes a computer gets the wrong orders and misbehaves, but even when things go wrong, it isn't out to get you.

The Computer Is the Means, Not the End

Most of us don't really want computers; we want the things computers do. When you're first learning about them, the task can be so absorbing and often so difficult that it seems as if just making your computer run is a worthy goal. But never forget that the goal is to get to know the computer so well that the information in it, not the computer itself, is the focus of your attention.

Computers Aren't Everything

Working with a computer can be a fascinating, exhilarating, frustrating, boring, or even terrifying experience. (You know you're really computing when it's two or three of these at the same time.) Learning to use one is a challenge, like getting to know somebody, climbing a mountain, or learning to play the violin. But it is a tool, that's all. The next time you start feeling overwhelmed because the computer lost your airplane reservation or ate your expense report, think about the things that really make life worth living — things like love, friendship, nature, and creativity. These things were all happening long before computers came along, and they haven't changed much since then.

Computers haven't changed the things that make us human. They never will.

About This Book

There are lots of excellent books about which button to press on a particular computer or which command does what in a particular program. This book is not one of them. It explains computers and the computing experience in general, so you'll be able to put any particular computer or program in its proper perspective. It covers

- what you need to know about computers and why
- what computers are and how they work
- how to choose a computer and the software for it
- how to unpack, set up, and learn to use a computer
- what things can go wrong with a computer and how to prevent them from happening
- how the most common kinds of computer programs work and how to use them most effectively
- how to stay out of trouble and how to get out of it when you don't
- what to do as time goes by and your computer isn't the latest thing anymore.

How to Use This Book

This book moves from the basics of how computers work, through buying, learning about, and setting one up, into more specific information about each of the major kinds of computer programs. Each chapter is divided into short, self-contained essays, so you can jump into any chapter anywhere.

If you're new to computing or you don't understand how a computer works, it's best to start at the beginning. Even if you're not new to computing, you'll probably learn a lot about computers by first skimming from the beginning to the end.

The first chapter is about how computers work in general. This is a good orientation for novices, but it also fills in some gaps in understanding if you've just been getting by with your computer until now. Once you understand that all of these machines work more or less the same way, you'll be less intimidated by any particular computer or program.

Chapters 2 and 3 explain how computers and the major kinds of programs differ and how to decide which ones are best for you.

Chapter 4 is about setting up a computer. Most people pay little attention to how and where they put up their machine, and this can result in a lot of needless discomfort and even injuries. Read this chapter before you set up your new computer, or to get advice on how to adjust your setup for greater comfort.

Chapter 5 presents a structured approach to learning how to use a computer. There are few shortcuts, but there are many distractions that can make learning more arduous and time-consuming than it needs to be. Read this chapter to find out how to learn what you need to know as quickly and effectively as possible.

Chapter 6 presents general rules of thumb you can follow to avoid problems with your computer. Most computer problems are manmade; it pays to learn how to avoid them.

Chapters 7 through 10 cover the four most common kinds of programs people use for work. Read the beginnings of these chapters to learn what word-processing, spreadsheet, database, and communications programs do. If you're already using one of these programs, check the topics later in the chapter for tips on how to use it better.

Chapter 11 offers step-by-step advice on diagnosing and resolving problems on your computer.

Chapter 12 addresses the inevitable march of technology and tells you what to do as your computer ages.

Computing has its own vocabulary. Dozens of terms in this book will be totally new to you or will have unfamiliar meanings when applied to computing. Each of these terms is printed in italic type the first time it appears, along with a simple definition. However, if you need a quick reference to any word's definition, check the glossary at the back of the book.

What You'll Learn

I've been using personal computers for a dozen years, during which I've learned many basic truths about computing. I've learned that a computer is a servant, not a master, and that it has a place in my life and work, but only a place. I've learned to appreciate the power of computers without fearing their complexity. I've learned the joy of working with information in the ways a computer allows.

This book will teach you what I've learned.

Charles Rubin
Sedona, Arizona
June 1994

**The Little Book of
Computer Wisdom**

CHAPTER 1

About Computers

Your Basic Computer System

The first step toward computer wisdom is understanding in general what computers are and how they work. Once you realize that all computers work the same way, they don't seem quite so mysterious.

Computers process information. They let us store, retrieve, and manipulate words, numbers, facts, pictures, sounds, and even video.

A computer system includes *hardware*, the parts you see and touch, and *software*, the instructions, or programs, that tell the hardware how to behave. Let's look at the hardware first.

Most computers today include a *system unit*, *disk drives*, a *monitor*, a *keyboard*, and a *mouse*. Usually a computer setup also includes a *printer* and perhaps a *CD-ROM drive* and a *modem*. In a *desktop* computer, each of these items comes in a separate box, and all of them have to be plugged together properly (like a stereo system) before you can use them. In a portable, or *laptop*, computer, the monitor, system unit, keyboard, and disk drives are all in one box.

The system unit is built around a central processing unit, or *CPU*. In personal computers, the CPU is a *microprocessor chip*, such as the Intel 80486 or the IBM PowerPC. The CPU is the brains of the computer, the chip that controls the other chips and processes instructions and information.

Other chips get information to or from the CPU. The most important of these are a *ROM* chip and *RAM* chips. The ROM chip contains permanent instructions; the RAM stores information temporarily, and only as long as the computer is turned on.

The CPU, ROM, and RAM chips usually come on a big piece of plastic called a *logic board*. Along with a couple of dozen chips, the logic board contains

- a *clock/calendar chip*, so the computer knows what time and day it is;
- *input/output ports*, where you plug in a printer, modem, or other components; and
- *expansion slots*, where you can plug in extra *circuit boards* to expand the computer's memory or add other capabilities.

In addition to the logic board, the system unit contains a power supply; a *video board*, which supplies a video signal to the monitor; an audio speaker; and one or more disk drives. Disk drives are used to store computer information. There are three common types.

Floppy disk drives use removable 3½-inch or 5¼-inch disks. They are called "floppy" because they're made of flexible plastic. Five-and-a-quarter-inch disks come inside a permanent paper or Mylar binding that has a slot in it so the disk drive can read or write information on the plastic disk inside. These floppy disks usually come in paper sleeves to protect them; you take each disk out of its sleeve like a record before you put it into the disk drive. Three-and-a-half-inch floppy disks, in contrast, come inside a permanent plastic shell, which has a sliding door that moves out of the way to expose the flexible disk inside when you insert the disk into a disk drive.

Floppy disks are convenient because you can always buy more of them when you need more storage space, but each disk holds only a few hundred pages of data. They are also the most popular way to transfer information from one computer to another: you store information on a floppy disk, take it out of your computer, and put it in another computer and use the information there.

Most *hard disk drives* aren't removable. The disk in a hard disk drive is made of aluminum and can store far more information than a floppy disk. A hard disk is your computer's storeroom — it can store tens of thousands of pages of data. In *removable hard disk drives,* the aluminum hard disks come in removable plastic cases. These drives combine the convenience of floppy disk drives with the capacity of small hard disk drives. Each removable hard disk can contain from twenty to forty thousand pages of data.

CD-ROM drives play removable, prerecorded compact disks that look like audio CDs but contain computer data. A single CD-ROM disk can store as much as two or three typical hard disk drives.

What Happens When You Start a Computer

Starting up a computer can be a little disconcerting if you've never done it before. You flip the power switch, the computer makes strange beeps and burps, a bunch of messages flash on the screen, and lights flash on and off on the front of the system unit. Finally this little show is over and you see a blinking light or a bunch of little pictures on the screen as the computer waits for you to tell it what to do next.

Here's what's really going on.

When you turn the computer on, the CPU chip wakes up, but it doesn't have a clue about what to do because it doesn't have any instructions. The CPU checks the ROM chip and then

Of Disks, Files, and Other Storage Matters

All computer information is stored as binary digits, or *bits* — in other words, zeroes and ones. Computers work through the opening and closing of millions of switches, or *gates*. A zero tells the computer to close a switch, and a one tells it to open a switch. On the earliest computers, people actually had to flip dozens of mechanical switches to set up the machine to make different calculations, but these days the software does the switch-flipping for us.

It takes eight bits to describe one letter or number, so eight bits, or a *byte*, is the basic unit of information in a computer. Disk storage is measured in *kilobytes* (thousands of bytes) or *megabytes* (millions of bytes). Most floppy disks can store about one megabyte, or 500 single-spaced pages of text. A hard disk sold with a typical computer can store from 100 to 500 megabytes. A CD-ROM disk can store 550 megabytes.

Any named collection of data or instructions on a disk is called a *file*. When you compose a letter on a computer and save it on a disk, the saved letter is a file. The program you might use to write that letter is also stored as a file. Each file has a unique name so you can tell which is which. (When you open a file and work with it on the screen, it is often called a *document*.)

Disks can contain dozens, hundreds, or even thousands of files, and when they do, it can be hard to find the one you want. To make things easier, disks are usually subdivided into named areas called *directories* or *folders*. Just as you can put some paper files in one folder or drawer and other files in another, you can divide a disk into directories or folders and store groups of different files inside each one.

reads, or *loads,* the instructions etched into it. The ROM instructions tell the CPU to play a sound or beep through the system unit's speaker, turn on the video circuitry (so you can see what's happening on the monitor), check the RAM chips to make sure they're working properly, and check the system unit's disk drives for a disk containing further instructions. All of this happens within a couple of seconds.

On some computers, the CPU always checks the floppy disk drives first. You hear each disk drive start up temporarily with a grinding noise as the CPU looks for instructions. A light flashes on each disk drive as the CPU checks it. If one of the floppy disk drives contains a disk that has the right instructions, the CPU reads those instructions and stores them in RAM (the CPU's temporary memory). Then it gets ready to receive further instructions from you.

If there are no disks in the floppy drives or none of them contains the right instructions, the computer checks its hard disk drive and usually finds the proper instructions there. Some computers are smart enough to look for instructions on the hard disk drive first, so you won't hear the floppy disk drives grind at all as the computer starts up.

After the computer loads its startup instructions from a disk, it waits for further commands from you. If it doesn't find the proper start-up instructions on a disk, it displays an error message or simply sits there.

The Computer Is the Software

A computer is just an expensive doorstop unless you give it instructions. What the computer does, what you see on the screen, and how you control the computer depends on what instructions — what software or *program* — is running at the time. You don't really learn to use a computer; you learn to use its software.

There are two basic kinds of software at work in personal computers.

The *operating system* is the software the CPU looks for on a disk after reading the instructions from the ROM chip. The operating system brings the computer fully to attention and prepares it to do your bidding. You and the CPU both use the operating system to manage the computer's hardware. For example, you can use the operating system to

- *format* a disk, or prepare it to store data
- display a list of files stored on a disk
- copy, move, rename, or erase files on a disk

- create, delete, rename, or erase directories or folders on a disk
- open, or *run,* an application program
- change the time or date on the computer's clock/calendar
- find out how much RAM, or memory, the computer has
- tell the computer how and where your modem or printer is connected to the system unit.

Application programs, or simply *applications,* are the software you use to handle your own work. A word-processing application lets you write letters or memos, for instance. A spreadsheet application enables you to make calculations. When we talk about using a computer to do our work, we really mean using an application program.

The Operating System Is the Computer's Personality

Although there are some differences in computer hardware, it's the operating system that really distinguishes one computer from another. An *IBM-compatible,* or *PC-compatible,* computer is IBM-compatible because it runs the *PC-DOS, MS-DOS,* or *OS/2* operating system. (Incidentally, the *DOS* in MS-DOS stands for *d*isk *o*perating *s*ystem.) A *Macintosh* is a Macintosh because its operating system is the *Macintosh Sys-*

tem. The operating system determines how a computer looks and feels — it's the connection, or *interface,* between you and the computer.

Ten years ago, all computer operating systems had *command line interfaces.* When the computer started up and waited for further instructions from you, all you saw was a prompt, like A:\>. You had to remember exactly what to type — commands such as RUN, TYPE, DIR, COPY, or MKDIR — to work with files or disks. The MS-DOS and PC-DOS operating systems have a command line interface like this.

These days, most computers have a *graphical user interface,* or *GUI* (pronounced *gooey*). A GUI makes a computer easier to use because it displays most of the possible commands and options right on the screen. You just choose the one you want by pointing to it with a mouse or *trackball* (see below).

The graphical user interface for the MS-DOS operating system is called *Microsoft Windows.* The Macintosh GUI is called the *Finder.*

**The Operating System Is Always Running,
But You Work with One Program at a Time**

After the computer has started up, you can use the operating system to perform computer housekeeping chores, or you can use it to run an application program. When you're running an application program, the commands you type or the mouse movements you make control that program. For example, if you're running a word-processing program and you press letter keys, the letters appear on your screen.

But even when you're using an application program, the operating system is still at work in the background. The application relies on the operating system to find out which disks are available, which printer to use, and other basic information about the state of the computer's hardware. When you print a letter from a word-processing program, for example, the program relies on the operating system to send that letter to your printer.

On older computers, you had to close, or quit, an application program in order to work with the operating system. If you were writing a letter and you wanted to use the operating system to make a new disk directory, you had to close the letter-writing program before you could use the operating system. In today's Windows or Macintosh computers, however, you can switch from an application program to the operating system without having to close the application. It's like changing channels on a television: the channel you just switched away from is still being broadcast, but you're not looking at it.

In fact, you can often run two or more applications and switch among them and the operating system.

When you work with a computer, it's important to remember where you are — whether you're working in the operating system or in an application program — because you can press the same keys and get very different results, depending on which program you're working in at the time. See Chapter 6 for more information.

Your Basic GUI

Whether you use Windows or the Finder, a graphical user interface has many of the same basic operating characteristics. Let's have a look.

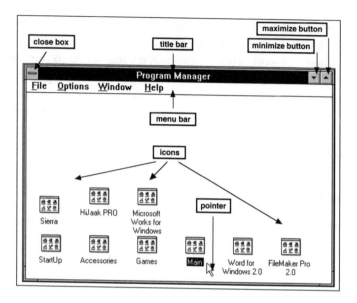

If you're running Microsoft Windows, you see a screen like the one above after the computer has finished starting up. The Program Manager *window* is open. Each window has a *title bar*, which identifies it, and a *menu bar* below the title bar, which contains the names of *menus*. Inside the window are *icons*. Surrounding this window on the screen is a blank area called the *desktop*.

On Macintosh computers, the menu bar is at the very top of the screen. The windows and the desktop appear below it.

Selecting. The whole idea behind using a GUI is to point to things, select them, and then work with them. You can't work with anything unless you point to it and select it first. You can tell when you have selected something because it darkens, changes color, or looks different from similar items around it. In the example above, we can tell that the Main icon has been selected because its name is darkened.

Notice the *pointer* next to the Main icon. To select something, you move the mouse on your desk (which moves the pointer), point to the item you want to select, and press, or *click*, the mouse button to select that item.

Managing windows. To close a window, you click its *close box*. To shrink a window to icon size, you click the minimize button. To make an icon-sized window full-size again, you click the maximize button. (On the Macintosh, a zoom box replaces these buttons.)

Opening an icon. Each icon in this window is a container for other icons. In some cases, an icon represents a program or a file, and when you open it, the program runs or the file opens. The fastest way to open an icon is to point to it and double-click the left mouse button — click it twice quickly. (On the Macintosh, the mouse has only one button.)

Using menu commands. The menus in the menu bar contain *commands* that let you work with selected items in various ways. For example, if you didn't want to open the Main icon in the window by double-clicking, you could open it by using the File menu's Open command:

1. Point to and click on the Main icon in the Program Manager window to select it.
2. Point to the File menu name and hold down the mouse button. The menu appears, like this:

3. Hold the mouse button down and move the pointer to the Open command. Its name darkens to show that you have selected it, like this:

New...	
Open	Enter
Move...	F7
Copy...	F8
Delete	Del
Properties...	Alt+Enter
Run...	
Exit Windows...	

Notice the command names on the menu above. *Keyboard shortcuts,* which are ways to choose the command from your keyboard instead of pointing with the mouse, appear to the right of many of them. For example, to choose the Open command on the above menu, you could press the Enter key.

4. Release the mouse button. The Main icon will open, like this:

As you can see, the Main window opens on top of the Program Manager window. Inside the Main window, the File Manager icon is selected.

Working with a window. There are many different ways to work with windows and their contents. Let's take a closer look.

- You can move the window on the desktop by pointing to its title bar, holding down the mouse button, and moving the pointer somewhere else. The window moves with it. This is called *dragging* a window. You can also drag items inside windows.

- You can close the window by clicking its close box.
- You can shrink or expand the window by clicking its maximize and minimize buttons (or its zoom box, if you're using a Macintosh).
- You can resize the window by dragging its edges (or dragging the *size box* on Macintosh windows).

Scrolling a window. Windows don't always show everything they contain. A hard disk window might contain dozens or hundreds of items, and it might not be large enough to show them all at once. In that case, the window is like a peephole into a larger area.

When a window contains more items that it can display all at once, its right and bottom edges have *scroll bars* that you can use to view different items. For example, here's a typical window from a Macintosh:

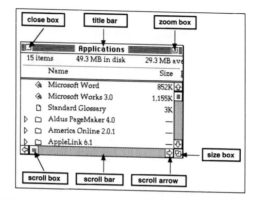

The right scroll bar moves you up and down inside the window; the bottom one moves you left and right. You can

- click a *scroll arrow* at one end of a scroll bar to move the view a little in that direction.
- drag a *scroll box* to move proportionally through the window's contents. For example, drag the box halfway across the scroll bar to display the middle part of the list.
- click in the gray part of the scroll bar to move one window's height or width at a time.

Moving or copying items. You can move or copy items inside or between windows by dragging them. For example, you might want to move the Standard Glossary file in the window above into the folder called Aldus PageMaker 4.0. To do this, you would select the Standard Glossary icon and drag it onto the Aldus PageMaker 4.0 folder. When you release the mouse button, the Standard Glossary icon will disappear inside the Aldus PageMaker 4.0 folder.

Using dialog boxes. Sometimes you have to choose among options or supply more information before a menu command can be carried out. The computer uses a *dialog box* to get this information from you. Commands that produce dialog boxes have ellipses (...) after their names. In Microsoft Works for Windows, for example, the Save As... command's dialog box looks like this:

Microsoft Works needs to know the name of the file you're saving and the place where you want to save it, so it displays this dialog box. To supply this information, you

1. type a file name in the File Name entry box (Works has suggested the name *word1*);
2. choose the disk where you want to save the file from the Drives menu;
3. choose a directory on the selected disk by clicking on its folder icon in the Directories list;
4. choose a file type option from the Save File as Type menu; and
5. click the OK button to save the file.

Some dialog boxes also have *checkboxes* you use to choose

Partisan Aside: All GUIs Aren't Created Equal

Apple Computer pioneered graphical user interfaces for personal computers. The Finder was introduced with the very first Macintosh, in January 1984. Microsoft Windows was in development at the time, but it wasn't perfected and widely used for another five years.

Macintoshes used to be far easier to use than computers running under MS-DOS, and in many ways they still are. Most people think that the Windows GUI makes an MS-DOS computer as easy to use as a Macintosh, but this just isn't so, in my opinion. The Finder is an integral part of the Macintosh operating system. In comparison, Windows is a smiley-face button slapped on top of MS-DOS. This makes for many important differences.

For example, each time you insert a floppy disk into a Macintosh, its icon immediately appears in the Finder, because the operating system knows that the disk has been inserted. Under Windows, you must choose a command or click an icon to tell the computer to check the disk drive, because MS-DOS doesn't have a clue as to what's in a floppy disk drive unless you specifically ask it to look.

Some people don't care about the differences between using Windows and using a Macintosh, but don't let anyone tell you the systems are the same. Try them both and choose for yourself.

options. When you click a checkbox, an X appears in it to show that the option is selected.

These are the key elements of a GUI. It is much easier to point, select, and click or choose menu or dialog box options than to remember commands and type them. The specific behavior of mouse clicks, menus, and dialog boxes can vary between Windows and the Macintosh Finder, but this is basically how things work.

How a GUI Enforces Consistency

GUIs would be great if all they did was make it easier to use the computer's operating system, but they do more than that. The system of pointing to menus, icons, and dialog boxes in windows to control the computer's operating system also extends to any application programs you run when the GUI is running.

On a Macintosh, every program takes advantage of the GUI, because the Finder GUI is the only way to control the Mac operating system. When you run Windows on a PC-compatible computer, any program you buy that is made to work with Windows will also use icons, menus, and windows. However, lots of PC-compatible programs work with MS-DOS or PC-DOS alone and don't use icons and windows.

The basic look of windows and icons is the same under a given GUI — windows, menus, dialog boxes, and icons always behave the same way. In fact, many commands that are common to every program (Open, Save, and Print, for example) appear on the File menu in every program. This makes it much easier to become comfortable with any program.

CHAPTER 2

Which Computer?

To Compute, or Not to Compute?

Buying a computer is not a trivial matter. It requires a significant investment of money and time. Before you run off and shop for a computer, make sure you're buying one for the right reasons.

Some people buy a computer to do things they weren't doing before. For example, there are thousands of computer games that aren't available on simpler, less expensive systems like Genesis and Nintendo. But most people buy a computer to do what they're already doing — writing letters, balancing their checkbook — more quickly or conveniently. Essentially, computers allow us to work with more information more efficiently than we otherwise could.

Computers improve productivity by storing and recalling large amounts of information much faster than a person can, and by transmitting large amounts of information to other places much faster than a person can. The important phrase here is "large amounts." A computer can't recall, print, or transmit one word any faster than you can. But it can print a ten-page letter in a fraction of the time it would take you to type it.

So the key to computer productivity is high-volume work. The more letters you have to write, the more a computer's speed will help you. The more research you have to do, the more time and money you'll save by doing it on your computer rather than driving around to various libraries.

Of course, a lot of people don't do high-volume work, or don't do it most of the time. In this situation, the computer probably costs you time. For example, I can look up, enter, or change an appointment in my good old Week-at-a-Glance book much faster than I can start up my computer, open a calendar program, and check the appointment there.

To help you decide whether to compute or not, consider the following reasons for buying a computer.

Good Reasons

- You need to store or manage a lot of information, and the computer will help you do it better. You should have a specific information-based task in mind, like writing or accounting.

- You want to do something you can't do at all without a computer — play computer games, for example, or gain access to data stored on disks or on other computers.
- You don't have a particular task in mind, but you're genuinely interested in learning about computers as a hobby.

Bad Reasons
- You think you should become "computer literate" so you won't be left behind, even though you don't want to do anything in particular with a computer.
- You write three letters a year and want to type them on a computer instead of on your old Remington.
- You want to impress your friends.

Before you make the leap to computing, be honest with yourself about your reasons for doing so.

What Do You Want to Do?

If you've decided to get a computer, you should have some idea of what you'll want to do with it. Computers can do hundreds of different things, depending on which programs you use and which components you buy, and it's easy to get carried away by

How About a Word Processor?

If your only reason for wanting a computer is to write an occasional letter, consider getting a word processor instead. A word processor is a computer that is set up just for writing. These machines are made by Brother, Smith-Corona, and other typewriter companies. They're less expensive than a regular personal computer, and they're easier to learn to use. Moreover, most word processors create files that are compatible with computer word-processing programs, so you can share your word-processor files with your computer-using friends and associates.

all that capability. But the only jobs that really matter are the ones you want to do. Do you want to

- write letters or other typed documents?
- prepare a budget, estimate loan costs, or make other financial calculations?
- store names and addresses and make mailing labels?
- keep track of your accounting?
- draw or paint with a computer?
- exchange information with other computer users?

Before you go shopping, make a list of the jobs you want to do with your computer. The more specific you can be, the better. If you want to write, for instance, do you want to write letters, reports, or a book? If you want to store names and addresses, how many of them do you want to store? If you want to prepare budgets and charts, what kinds do you want to produce?

Most computers have enough memory and disk storage space to handle most of the common tasks that people are likely to do. But if you know you want to work with thousands of database records or dozens of color images, you'll need a larger hard disk, more memory, or both. If you want to prepare newsletters, drawings, or other documents, you may want a computer with a faster CPU, which can handle graphics more quickly, or a larger monitor than the one sold with most computers.

Take your needs list with you when you shop. Once you're in a store, you'll face a blizzard of different computers and different application programs. Features and specifications fly at you from all directions. Your list of needs is the compass that will guide you through the storm.

PC or Mac?

The two most common types of computer are PCs, or IBM-compatible computers, and Macintoshes, made by Apple Computer. At first glance, PCs and Macintoshes seem very much alike, but there are important differences between them. Let's look at some of the pros and cons of each type.

PC Pros

PCs are by far the most widely used computers in the world. They have been available since 1981, and at least 100 million of them are around today. They have been adopted as the standard personal computer by most of the world's large corporations.

The basic design of PCs is not a trade secret. Although IBM was the first company to make a PC, dozens of companies produce them today. In effect they are a commodity, and the price competition among companies is fierce. PCs offer a lot of computing power for the buck.

Because so many PCs are being used, many more software programs are available for PCs than for Macs, and there are also many more accessories, books, magazines, and training materials. When companies come up with new personal-computer products or improved versions of their existing products, they usually do PC versions first, because the number of PC users, or the *installed base,* is so much larger than the number of Mac users. In many cases, the PC version of a program or accessory is the only version available; many companies don't bother to produce a Macintosh version because that market is so much smaller.

PC Cons

The operating system software for PCs is MS-DOS, which came out in 1981. Even then it was only a slight improvement on an even older operating system (CP/M, which came out in the mid-1970s). MS-DOS is a powerful operating system, but it's difficult to learn and use. It has a *command-line interface,* so you have to learn commands with strange names like MKDIR or SYSINFO, and you have to type them in properly or you get error messages that don't tell you what you've done wrong.

You can make a PC easier to use by running the Microsoft Windows graphical user interface along with MS-DOS (see "Your Basic GUI" in Chapter 1). However, Windows only puts a prettier face on some aspects of MS-DOS; it doesn't replace it. Sometimes you have to use MS-DOS commands anyway, and when you do, it's much harder to figure out what's going on than it is on a Macintosh.

Macintosh Pros

The Mac's main advantage is its remarkable ease of use. Macintosh computers are decidedly easier to use than PCs, even PCs running Windows (*Windows PCs,* for short). And don't take my word for it. A January 1994 study by the international consulting firm Arthur D. Little showed that people using Macintoshes finished a range of typical business computing tasks in roughly half the time it took people using Windows PCs. Furthermore, the Macintosh users in the study performed 85 percent of their tasks correctly, compared with only 43 percent of the Windows users.

The Macintosh's graphical user interface is better than Windows because it controls the computer's hardware more directly. For example, you can use the Macintosh Finder to assign more than the normal amount of memory for a particular program to use, but you have to use an MS-DOS command to do this on a PC.

Finally, it's much easier to add memory or other capabilities to a Macintosh than it is to a PC. Most of the time, you simply plug something in and the Mac automatically recognizes the new capability. On a PC, you have to type a bunch of MS-DOS commands to let the computer know you've made a change.

Macintosh Cons

Apple Computer, Inc., is the only company that makes Macintoshes, and since most businesses don't want to rely on just one company to provide their computers, they don't choose

Macs as their standard computer. Until recently, Macs were also more expensive than PCs.

There are only about a tenth as many Macintoshes in the world as there are PCs, so there aren't as many programs, books, accessories, and training aids available for the Macintosh.

Finally, while the Macintosh can use data files or floppy disks created on a PC, this requires a few extra steps, such as running a special program to recognize PC disks or run PC software.

So how to choose? Necessity is the fastest way to answer that question. Many businesspeople buy a PC or a Mac because it's the only computer that does what they need. So ask yourself, *Do I need a particular program that only runs on one type of computer, or do I need to use the same computer as the people I work with?* If so, then get that computer.

For example, if your accountant insists that you use an accounts-receivable program that only runs on a Macintosh, then get a Mac. If you work in an office and everyone there is using PCs, get a PC.

If you don't need a particular computer for one of these reasons, then get the computer that seems easiest to use and that works in the way that's most comfortable for you. How do you tell?

First, see for yourself. No matter how enthusiastic somebody else may be about one type of machine or the other, try them out for yourself. Decide what you want to do with a computer, then visit computer stores and ask for demonstrations of those things on both kinds. Visit several different stores and get demonstrations of different computers and types of programs. Ask the salespeople to explain why one computer is better than others. You'll hear conflicting recommendations; each salesperson will have some reason why a particular computer is better. But if you talk to enough people, you'll develop a sense of what's best for you.

Second, ask lots of other people. If you can, visit computer user groups in your area. These groups are usually specific to PCs, Macintoshes, or other kinds of computers. Visit more than one group to see different computers in action and talk to people who use them every day. Ask coworkers and friends what they like or dislike about their computers. Be sure to ask about any problems they've had and how difficult they were to solve.

Once you've made the basic decision between PC and Mac, you're ready to go shopping in earnest.

Choosing a Printer

A computer system really isn't complete without a printer, so include the cost of a printer in your budget when you shop. These days, there are three types of printers to consider.

Dot matrix printers form letters and numbers one at a time by pressing a group of pins against an inked ribbon. A dot matrix printer usually has either nine or twenty-four pins in its print head. The pins are arranged in a square grid, or matrix, and different pins push against the ribbon in different patterns to form different characters. A twenty-four-pin printer forms smoother characters. These printers accept either single-sheet paper or *continuous* (fan-fold) *paper*, which comes in one long strip. You separate individual pages after they're printed by tearing them off along perforations.

Dot matrix printers are compact and inexpensive. Some models sell for less than $200, and those with better print quality range up to about $500. However, dot matrix printers are noisier than other types, and their print quality isn't the best.

Ink jet printers make characters by spraying ink in different patterns onto paper. Overall, these printers offer better printing quality than dot matrix printers, they're quiet, and they cost only slightly more than dot matrix printers. They accept single-sheet paper only. You can buy a black-and-white ink jet printer for about $300, and you can get one that prints in color for less than $750. Ink jet printers are also quite reliable. Canon, Hewlett Packard, and Apple Computer even sell portable ink jet printers that weigh less than ten pounds.

The only drawbacks to ink jet printers are that they're fairly slow, printing one or two pages per minute at best, and their ink sometimes smears when you print on glossy paper.

Laser printers print like photocopy machines. They fuse powdered ink (toner) with paper through a heat transfer process. These are the fastest printers, producing from four to twelve pages per minute, and they produce the best print and graphics. However, laser printers are also the most expensive, ranging from about $700 up to several thousand dollars for models that produce typeset-quality printing or color. Laser printers are also larger and heavier than ink jet and dot matrix printers.

If you're on a tight budget or have limited space, an ink jet or dot matrix printer is fine for personal or small business use, but if you'll be printing long documents or lots of graphics, or you want desktop-publishing quality, go for a laser printer. You won't regret it.

What About Buying Used?

If you have sticker shock from new computer prices and you simply want a system to write a few personal letters, keep a budget, or store some names and addresses, you can save big by buying used. A brand-new computer will have more power and more storage than a used one and will be better able to run the latest programs, but none of this may matter to you.

Since new computer models appear almost monthly, used computers depreciate rapidly. You can buy a two-year-old computer for half what you'd pay for a new one, and it may meet your needs just as well. You can find three-year-old PCs or Macs with printers and software for under $500. Older computers cost as little as $150.

Here are some tips about buying a used computer.

Look for a package deal. Check the local newspaper for classified ads. Try to find a deal in which you get a printer and a few application programs along with the computer. You'll be buying a system that has been working for the person who used it, so you won't have to worry about matching a computer from one source with a printer from another and software from a third. Also, you can often get software worth hundreds or thousands of dollars for nothing. Try to get the original manuals and software installation disks with any hardware or software you buy.

Make sure the computer can run the software you want. If you want to use a specific version of a specific program, make sure it will run on the used computer you're considering. Most used computers don't come with the current version of the operating system and any application programs, but unless the computer is more than three years old, it should be able to run the latest software.

If you'll be using the computer only to write a few letters or track some personal data, you may not need the latest version of the operating system or any programs you use. Many people still use computers and programs that were made in the 1980s. However, if you need to share files with others who are using the current version of a particular application program, then you should make sure the used computer can run the same version.

In general, the previous generation of computer models can still run the latest software, even if they don't come with it. For example, a 386-based PC or a 68030-based Mac may come with older operating systems such as Microsoft Windows 3.0, MS-DOS version 5, or Macintosh System 6, but it's powerful enough to run the latest versions of these operating systems if you choose to upgrade. In contrast, older computers (286-based PCs and 68020-based Macs, for example) won't run the newest versions of the operating system software.

Test-drive the system. When you check out a used computer, start it up, run a few programs on it, and try out the printer to make sure it works. If you don't know how to do these things, take along a friend who does.

Reregister the software. If the used system you buy comes with application programs, write to the programs' makers and register as the current user. Look for each program's serial number on the labels of the original master disks or inside the manual and include this number and the program's version number in your letter. Tell each maker that you purchased the program used and now want to register as the owner. This way, you'll officially become eligible for technical support, and you'll be notified about upgrades to the program in the future.

Scout out support systems. You'll probably buy a used computer from an individual, not a company. If the computer is a name brand such as Compaq, IBM, or Apple, you can usually still get support for it from the manufacturer. Look inside the manual that came with the computer and find out what number to call if you're in trouble. If you're new to computing or if you're buying an off-brand computer, join a local user group so you can rely on it for general support or to help solve any problems you may have.

Salespeople Recommend What They Know

Hundreds of different computers are available, but the economics of computer retailing prohibit any store from carrying very many of them. In fact, out of all the different computers that are made, most stores carry the same handful of brands. Does this mean those brands are the best? No. It just means they have better distribution channels or their makers offered a lower wholesale price than the competition did.

Many fine computers sell poorly because they don't get the distribution they need. There's only a certain amount of shelf space, and the good guys don't always get it. But salespeople can sell only what they carry, so it's not surprising that no matter what your problem is, their computer is the best answer. As the saying goes, "When the only tool you have is a hammer, everything looks like a nail."

Don't confine your search to the half-dozen machines you see at one store. Shop around. Ask around. Read the articles in computer magazines that compare makes and models. Check with user groups.

A brand you won't easily find may be a little faster or more reliable than one you'll see everywhere. In fact, some of today's best computer buys aren't in any store, because they're sold only through mail order.

What Makes Hardware Different

After you've decided whether to buy a PC or a Mac, you'll have to zero in on a particular model. Most people do the same things with a computer — a little writing, a little bookkeeping, a few games. Virtually any personal computer will handle these tasks. So why are there so many different computer setups, and why should you care?

Different computer setups, or configurations, are suited for different kinds of work. Working with a simple line drawing is much less taxing on a computer's resources than working with a video image, for example.

Let's have a look at the basic differences in configurations and how they affect the computer's ability to help you perform different tasks.

The Processor Chip, or CPU

Every PC runs on a processor designed by Intel Corporation, although over the years new models of the processor have replaced older ones. The original PC processor was the Intel

8088. In 1984, the IBM PC AT computer used a newer chip, the 80286 (286 for short). Since then, there have been 80386 (386) and 80486 (486) chips, and now there's one called the Pentium. Next year there will be another new one with a different name.

Macintosh computers use processors from Motorola, designated 68000, 68020, 68030, and 68040. The newest Macs use a new processor from IBM and Motorola called the PowerPC, whose models are designated 601, 603, 604, and so on.

The higher the number in a series, the newer and faster the chip. These days, you'll only find new PCs with 386, 486, and Pentium chips. Today's Macs use 68040 and PowerPC chips. But each chip comes in different flavors. Intel processors come in SX and DX versions. The less expensive SX version doesn't do math calculations as quickly as the DX, because it lacks a math-processing unit, or *floating point unit.* Some Macintoshes have a cheaper 68040 processor called the 68LC040, which also lacks a floating point unit.

The Processor Speed, or Clock Speed

Processor speed is measured in *megahertz* (MHz), or millions of cycles per second. A faster clock speed is better, but only when you're comparing the same generation of processor. For example, a 50 MHz 486 is definitely faster than a 25 MHz 486, but a 33 MHz 386 is not faster than a 25 MHz 486. The older processor, the 386, may have a faster clock speed, but the newer, 486 processor is more efficient and can perform tasks more quickly at lower clock speeds. A newer generation of chip is nearly always faster than an older generation.

The faster the processor, the more expensive the machine. Some jobs you do on a computer make the processor work harder than others. Writing letters is a slam-dunk for any computer, so the processor speed won't matter much, but if you want to draw or paint in color or you have large amounts of numbers or facts to calculate or sort, a faster processor will make your work go more quickly. If you think you'll need a faster processor, look for a computer whose processor has a built-in floating point unit to speed up mathematical calculations.

To simplify your search, choose the processor first, then decide which clock speed you want. For example, a 386-based PC or a 68030-based Mac is fine for word processing, but you'll need the extra horsepower of a 486, Pentium, 68040, or Power-PC chip if you're working with lots of graphics, video, or large amounts of numbers.

The Amount of RAM
RAM is measured in kilobytes (KB) or megabytes (MB). Most PCs these days have from one to eight megabytes of RAM.

RAM keeps getting less expensive, and programs keep hogging more of it. Ten years ago, personal computers had between 64K and 640K of RAM and programs fit the available space. Now, most computers have at least 4MB of RAM, and a typical word-processing program might use 2MB by itself. Very soon, the minimum setup on any computer will be 8MB or even 16MB of RAM. What's true of RAM is also true of hard disks. Ten years ago, a 40MB hard disk was a real monster. Today, it's not unusual to see 250 or 500MB hard disks, and they cost less than the 40MB disks of a decade ago.

Computers are typically sold with enough RAM to run one program at a time. On a PC, you'll get at least 1MB of RAM. If you plan to run Windows, you should get at least 4MB. On a Macintosh, you'll get at least 4 or 8MB of RAM, depending on the model. If you plan to work with large drawings or paintings, or if you want to be able to run several programs at a time, buy a computer with at least 8MB of RAM.

The Amount of Hard Disk Storage

Hard disks today come in sizes measured in megabytes. Most PCs have hard disks with 100 to 500 megabytes of storage.

Most space on a computer's hard disk is used by the operating system, GUI, and application programs. In most cases, a standard hard disk of 100MB or more will be more than adequate unless you plan to store more than a half-dozen programs or lots of large drawings, paintings, layouts, or other data files. (Graphics files tend to take up a lot of room.)

The Video Output

The video output capabilities of PCs are standardized, but there are different standards. All PCs produce color video these days. The old color standard was EGA (named after IBM's video board, which was called the Enhanced Graphics Adapter), and the current ones are VGA (after IBM's Video Graphics Array board) and Super VGA. The standard determines the resolution (sharpness), the number of colors, and the size of the video image the computer can display. Most current PCs provide Super VGA video. With Super VGA, it's important for the computer to have a special section of memory — video memory or video RAM — to maintain the image it's producing. The more RAM, the bigger and better the image. Look for a PC with at least one megabyte of video RAM.

Almost every computer produces color images, so that's not an issue. The real issue is the quality of the color and the size of the monitor you can use. Every personal computer will produce acceptable color images on a fourteen-inch monitor. However, if you're a graphic artist or you want to manipulate digital photographs, you'll want to display more colors and perhaps use a larger screen. Expanded video capabilities can get expensive ($1,000 to $3,000), so if you're new to computing, start with the standard setup and see how it goes. If you need the display space but not necessarily the color, you can get a larger black-and-white, or monochrome, monitor for considerably less — usually $500 to $1,000.

The Monitor

Although a computer might produce a video image of a certain quality, the monitor itself will ultimately determine what you see. Most PC monitors are color these days, but they vary in size, dot pitch, and video display technology.

A typical PC monitor has a fourteen- or fifteen-inch display. Larger monitors (up to twenty-one inches) are better if you need to see a lot of data at once, as with a large budget spreadsheet or a big newsletter layout.

The dot pitch is the space between each dot of light on the screen. Smaller dot pitches make for sharper images. A good PC monitor has a dot pitch of .28 millimeters or less (smaller numbers are better).

Video technology affects the way the picture is displayed.

Sony's Trinitron technology is considered one of the best, because it uses only one electron gun to produce the image; a garden-variety monitor uses three guns and typically produces a fuzzier image.

Again, the standard video system is good enough for most jobs. You may want a larger or higher-quality monitor if you work with detailed graphics or schematic drawings, but try the standard setup first.

Extra Goodies

CD-ROM drives are becoming very popular, and many computer systems come with one. Many PCs that have CD-ROM drives also come with an extra *sound board* that delivers better sound, along with a pair of external stereo speakers so the programs you play from a CD-ROM disk will sound better. (Macintoshes don't need an extra sound board, because they deliver great sound right out of the box.) Computers with a CD-ROM and extra sound gear are often billed as *multimedia* systems, because they're set up to give you great sound as well as a color video display.

To sum all this up, a typical PC at this writing might have a 486DX processor that runs at 50 MHz and be set up with four megabytes of memory, a 170-megabyte hard disk, Super VGA video output, and a fourteen-inch color monitor. A multimedia system would have a CD-ROM drive, a sound board (if it's a PC), and external stereo speakers.

Look for Reliability and Support

Every company in the personal computer business offers essentially the same computers as every other company. Manufacturers try to distinguish their systems by giving them fancy names, offering lower prices, or including different programs or accessories with the computer, but if computers have the same specifications, the main differences are reliability and the quality of the manufacturer's support for the product.

Computer magazines offer comparisons of different makes, and while you'll find some differences in performance among different brands with the same processor, the product's reliability, the warranty, and the maker's technical support will be much more important to your overall computing experience. Usually magazine reviewers try calling each maker's technical support number to evaluate the company's service and support.

In addition to checking computer magazine comparisons, ask your local user group to recommend specific brands based on real-world experience. Find a computer with a good reputa-

Because so many people are making PCs and so many stores are selling them, computer prices are fairly consistent from one retailer to another. Any differences between similarly configured systems will probably be minor. Don't let a couple of hundred dollars determine which computer you buy. Instead, consider the reputation of the manufacturer and the reliability of the store you buy it from.

tion, a good warranty, and good factory support. Everyone ends up needing help, and even if you have the fastest computer on the block, it's frustrating when that help is hard or impossible to come by.

Sexy Doesn't Necessarily Mean Satisfying

Some of the latest technologies are really impressive. Voice recognition, handwriting recognition, the ability to capture and play color video, and photographic-quality images are the sort of things that excite computer magazine editors. But do you need them?

I'm truly fascinated by laptop computers, for example, but I've never bought one, because I just can't imagine using one very much. I don't travel often, and I don't need a computer with me when I do. My heart still wants a laptop, because I think they're cool, but my head keeps vetoing the proposition.

Computer retailers often try to make an ordinary computer more attractive by bundling a bunch of extra goodies with it. They'll throw in a couple of games, or a sound board and a pair of speakers, or a CD-ROM drive with some games and an encyclopedia program.

Buying a computer bundled with extras is like buying the loaded model of a car. All those extras make the deal sound sweeter. But after you drive off the lot, you realize that electrically heated sideview mirrors or dual-zone climate control really aren't worth what you had to pay for them.

Before you're smitten by the extra goodies in a computer bundle and reach for your credit card, do a reality check. Ask yourself if you really want or need that extra doodad. Is it something you were planning to buy anyway? Remember that you can always add it later if you find you can't live without it.

Stay Off the Bleeding Edge

Computer and software companies are often in such a race to top one another that they release products before they have been fully tested. In effect, people who buy the first Megamunch PC with a brand-new kind of processor are living on the edge. They're paying to discover problems the manufacturer didn't bother to find or correct before the product was shipped. (To be fair, so many things can go wrong that manufacturers couldn't possibly discover them all unless they tested new computers for years. But all the same, most manufacturers ship products with known problems, because they want to beat the other guys to market.)

There have been notable problems with early versions of new processor chips, new versions of operating systems, and new versions of application programs. People who insist on being the first to have these products often spend hours working around such problems. Unless this is your idea of a good time, don't volunteer as a guinea pig. Don't buy a new product until a few months after it has come out. By then, some buyer who had to have the latest thing will have discovered the big problems, and the manufacturer will have corrected them in the version you buy.

How can you tell when it's safe to buy? Ask at user groups or check computer magazines for reports about problems and whether or not they've been fixed. Most computer magazines have news pages or columns that report these, and writers are just killing themselves to be the first to report a problem with a new product.

Another great source of problem reports is computer information services such as CompuServe, America OnLine, and Prodigy. Each of these services has special areas, or forums, in which users can report difficulties with different computers and software programs. Often services like this are the first place where such news surfaces. If you're new to computing, maybe you can ask a friend who uses one of these services to check for problem reports on the appropriate forum.

Don't Rush, But Don't Wait for the Perfect Deal

You probably won't get the same kind of buy-today pressure in a computer store that you get at some car dealerships, but the techno-sexiness of a new computer system sometimes makes people a little crazy. There have been times when I was willing to consider overdrawing my checking account or getting a cash advance on a credit card to buy a computer system. In the end, I took a more rational financial approach, and it didn't ruin the experience for me one bit.

But computers can foster irrational buying impulses. Normally, these come in two varieties: "Heaven won't wait," and "Heaven is just around the corner."

At any given time, any particular computer can seem like the deal of the century. But the chances are it isn't even the deal of the day. So many people are selling computers that you can nearly always find exactly the same deal in many different places. So don't let anyone (or your own lust for technology) sucker you into thinking you've got to make the deal today. If you wait a few weeks, there's an excellent chance that your deal of the century will get better, because computers are always getting faster and cheaper.

On the other hand, the steady progress in computers — more features, more power, and lower prices — often encourages people to wait too long. Things will always be better and cheaper, it's true. But while you're waiting, you're not computing. I took out a two-year loan for my first computer. I paid more for that computer than any I've bought since. But that computer made my life so much better that it would have been a bargain at twice the price.

Take a Test Drive

Incredible as it seems, lots of people decide to buy a computer without ever having actually tried it out. This defies common sense.

You wouldn't buy a car without driving it, because you'd want to make sure it doesn't handle like the *Queen Mary*. You wouldn't buy a house without walking around inside it first, because you'd want to make sure it has running water and other conveniences. If you buy a computer without trying it out first, you could end up having to live with a keyboard you hate or a monitor that seems fuzzy.

Once you've decided that you want a computer, be sure to try each of the models you're considering yourself. Here are some things to look for on a test drive:

- The keyboard and mouse are your main ways of working with the computer, so make sure they perform the way you want them to. Check for stiff keys, noisy keys, an awkward mouse shape, and poor tracking (when the pointer doesn't move smoothly or quickly on the screen when you move the mouse). If you're left-handed, make sure the mouse can be set up on the left side of the keyboard.
- Look at different monitors and try to notice differences in brightness, sharpness, and color values. Some monitors have better glare filtering than others. You'll spend a lot of time looking at the screen, so be sure to get the one that's easiest on your eyes.
- Try to notice how much noise the computer makes. A noisy computer can be really annoying. (I once had an extra-large monitor whose fan sounded like a vacuum cleaner.)
- Look for big differences in speed when you perform similar

operations on different computers. See how long it takes each computer to start up. If possible, try opening the same program or doing the same task on different computers. Different processors or clock speeds, different amounts of memory, and different hard disks can cause big differences in speed. If a computer seems a little slow in the store, it will seem glacial when you're trying to work with it at home.

- Test lots of computers. Don't just try one or two and make a decision. Try a handful at different stores until you get a sense of what you like and don't like.

Get a Basic Intro

If you buy from a computer dealer because you need the extra support, make sure you get it. Ask the dealer to give you a basic orientation to the computer system when you pick it up. Most computer store chains offer free orientation classes to new customers, and taking one will help you get up to speed on your new computer much more quickly. It will also acquaint you with the store's technical support people, so you'll know who to call if there's a problem.

CHAPTER 3

Which Software?

Applications Make the Computer Useful

An operating system wakes the computer up and makes it attentive to your commands, but you need application programs to make the computer perform specific tasks. Each application program lets you work with information in a different way. One might let you manipulate words, while another lets you make financial calculations. There are thousands of different application programs, and each of them enables you to make your computer do something a little different. If you try one application and you don't like it, you can buy another one and use it instead.

The only requirement is that you choose an application that is compatible with your computer's operating system and hardware setup. There are different programs, or different versions of the same program, for MS-DOS and Macintosh, for example. Even among programs for the same operating system, some require more memory or disk space than others.

(Usually the program's box lists its operating system and hardware requirements, or *system requirements.*)

The first step in deciding what application programs you'll need is to learn how the software universe is divided up. We can group all the thousands of different programs into a few categories.

Word-processing programs let you manipulate words. Basically, a word-processing program turns your computer into a sophisticated typewriter that allows you to store, retrieve, edit, and print written documents such as letters, reports, and books.

Spreadsheet programs let you make financial or other mathematical calculations and graph their results. If you want to prepare a budget and then make a pie chart showing how much of it you plan to spend on groceries, a spreadsheet is for you.

Database programs help you work with collections of facts, such as address lists, inventories, customer lists, and sales orders. With a database program, you can store, sort, select, and print groups of facts. For instance, if you use a database to store hundreds of sales orders, you can then sort them alphabetically by customer name, or print only the orders that total more than $500.

Communications programs link your computer with other computers so you can exchange information with them.

Graphics programs let you create and manipulate shapes and objects on your screen. Among graphics programs, *drawing programs* let you work with specific lines and shapes, *painting programs* let you draw or paint freehand, and *page layout programs* work like drawing programs, except the shapes become boxes that contain words and pictures on a page.

Integrated programs combine several applications into one. Programs such as Microsoft Works or ClarisWorks combine word-processing, spreadsheet, database, communications, and sometimes painting and drawing applications in one program. These programs are a good choice for beginners, because they introduce you to several software categories with just one program at a reasonable price.

Game programs turn your computer into something like a Nintendo or Genesis system, but the graphics, sound, and complexity of the games are usually much better. A typical computer is much more powerful than a game system and can run more sophisticated games.

Utility programs help you perform housekeeping chores, such as inspecting and repairing your disks, searching for information on disks, and protecting your computer from damage.

Educational programs help you learn about different subjects. Educational programs exist for most grade levels in elementary and secondary schools as well as for college and professional subjects. You can also buy reference programs, such as on-disk encyclopedias and dictionaries, and training programs that teach you how to use a certain computer program or perform a certain task.

Special-purpose programs perform a very specific job, such as accounting, project management, scientific modeling, and weather forecasting.

Of Programs, Documents, and Files

Some programs are self-contained: you start up the program and then play a game, learn a lesson, test a disk, or perform some other task that doesn't require you to create and save information. When we think of doing work with our computers, though, we usually think of using *productivity programs* to store important business or personal information.

All productivity programs let you create documents that contain the information you're working with. A productivity program without a document is like a pencil without paper: you have the means to process information but nowhere to do it.

When you first open one of these programs, you'll probably create a new document and enter your data in it. If you want to write a letter, for example, you'll open your word-processing program, use the program's File menu to open a new document, and then begin typing the letter in the document window on the screen. When you've finished typing, you can print the letter on paper.

When a document is displayed on your screen, it's stored in your computer's RAM, so if you were to shut the computer off, the document would disappear. To store it permanently, you save it as a file on a disk. Once you've saved the document to a disk, you can then put it away, or close it, to remove it from the screen. The next time you want to work with it, you open the file to display it again.

With a productivity program, you can create as many different documents as you like. You can store as many of them as your disk has room for. Many programs let you open more than one document at a time and then switch from one to another, just as you might have two or three pieces of paper on your desk and glance from one to another.

When you have finished working with a particular application, you put away any documents that are open (saving them to disk if you want to store them permanently), then close, exit, or quit the program itself.

Each Program Is an Island

Each program has its own way of recording documents as files on a disk. The method by which a file is saved is called the file *format*. If you save a document with a WordPerfect word-processing program, for example, the resulting file is in WordPerfect's unique, or *native*, file format, which is different from the file format used by Microsoft Word or any other program. Whenever you save a document in a program's native format, the file contains data (words or numbers) as well as information about what that particular program does with the data (how it looks on the screen, any calculations made on the data, and so on).

Computers wouldn't be very useful if people using different programs couldn't exchange files, however, so most programs can open files in other programs' native file formats. For example, if you're using Microsoft Word and you want to use a file that was created with WordPerfect, you can open that file — Microsoft Word will automatically translate the file from WordPerfect's native format into Microsoft Word's native format. And just to make sure you can really share your files with people using other programs, you can also save files in other programs' formats. For example, suppose you're using Microsoft Word and you want to share a file with somebody using

MacWrite, and suppose the MacWrite program can't automatically recognize Microsoft Word files. In this case, you can save the Microsoft Word file in MacWrite's format so MacWrite can open it.

Most programs within a category of software can open, or *import*, and save, or *export*, one another's native file formats. All the major word-processing programs can read one another's files, for example. However, programs from different categories can't read one another's files — that is, you can't use a word-processing program to read a spreadsheet program's native files.

People who use computers often need to move data from one kind of program to another. Maybe you need to include that column of numbers you stored in a spreadsheet file in a report you're creating with your word-processing program. To make these kinds of data exchanges possible, there's a universal file format that every program can read and write. That format is called *ASCII* (American Standard Code for Information Interchange), which is pronounced *asky*. In ASCII files, only the raw data (the letters and numbers) are saved, not the information about how the data are handled within a particular program. ASCII is also called *text format,* because it contains only letters and numbers, or text characters, not programming instructions.

It would be a lot simpler if all programs could save files in one standard format so we didn't have to go through all this importing and exporting. Software companies say they're working toward this kind of compatibility among programs, but I'm not optimistic. Each software designer thinks his or her program's format is the best, so it's hard to see how they'll all agree on just one.

Know What You Want to Do

Choosing the right software depends on matching your needs with the features and operating style of a program. This isn't as easy as finding the right wrench to fit a particular bolt; it's more like finding a car that suits your personal taste and driving habits.

People perform tasks; software performs functions. Software companies describe functions like data entry, formatting, and calculations. People talk about tasks like putting together a garage sale flyer or figuring out how much to save each month for Josephine's college fund. Software functions are easily categorized and explained, whereas people's tasks are varied and personal.

You can see which functions a program performs by reading promotional literature, talking to a salesperson, reading the product's box, thumbing through its manual, or browsing in a book about it. But those functions won't mean much to you unless you can weigh them against the things you want to do.

For example, you may want to write. That's pretty vague in software terms. It means you'll want a word processor, but that still leaves a lot of options. Some word-processing programs have features for indexing books, creating tables of contents, creating multicolumn layouts, and making outlines, but these will just be in your way if all you want to do is write letters.

If you're in business and you want to store sales records, you'll need a database program. But knowing the number of records you need to store in a month or a year and the variety of ways in which you want to sort, select, or print those records will help determine which database program you should choose.

Before you shop for software, sit down and list the kinds of projects you want to undertake with it. Try to be as specific as possible about what it is you want to do. If you still aren't sure what category of software you'll need to handle a particular project, ask around in software stores, at user group meetings, or among friends and coworkers.

As you zero in on the details of what you want to do, you'll find yourself asking more questions about how programs in a category differ from one another. Determine exactly what you want and take your time evaluating different programs. The time you spend will be worth it.

Software Is Personal

A computer is a machine, and software is the face of the machine. But using software isn't just clicking buttons and choosing commands, any more than driving a car is just pushing a pedal and turning a steering wheel. Each car has its own personality and feel; the same goes for software.

You might like the way a certain word-processing program lets you indent paragraphs, while somebody else might hate it. Or you might never think about that particular aspect of the program, just as many people don't really think about the precision (or lack of it) in a car's steering.

Among PC programs, for example, Microsoft Word for Windows became popular because it used menus and dialog boxes to change the appearance of text in a document, while WordPerfect, the market leader, required people to type formatting codes, which were a throwback to the dark ages of computing. People who were used to the formatting codes didn't mind them, but new computer users thought they were cumbersome. Now WordPerfect uses menus and dialog boxes too.

In the Macintosh market, Microsoft Word is sometimes criticized for being sluggish when it comes to checking spelling and performing some other tasks. WriteNow is much faster and uses less RAM, but Microsoft Word has more features (it can format mathematical equations, for instance). People who care a lot about speed end up using WriteNow for word processing, while those who need extra features use Microsoft Word.

The more experience you have with one category of program, the more easily you will be able to distinguish between one program's personality and another's. If you've used one word processor for months and then try another one, for example, you can immediately spot the difference in feel. But if you've never used a word processor at all, it is hard to tell what you like or don't like about any of them.

Experience counts. Get as much as you can. Once you've narrowed down your list of potential programs by comparing their listed features with the jobs you want to do, test-drive each of them to see which one feels the best.

Bigger Isn't Necessarily Better

Many a great program has started out lean, mean, and simple, only to bloat up in later versions. This is considered a sign of success in the software business. Carmakers do the same thing. Remember the original Thunderbird? Two seats, plenty of pep, fun to drive. A few years later it was a four-door, two-ton, rolling sofa.

Software designers get featuritis. They think that if the original program sells well, a new version that does more will sell even better. Unfortunately, they're usually right.

One reason that software gets more complex with each version is that corporate buyers, who buy most of the productivity programs, have little checklists of required features. These checklists are developed by committees, which are often made up of people whose main goal is to avoid blame and embarrassment. As far as most corporate checklist-making committees are concerned, the more features, the merrier. After all, if Ms. Big discovers that she can't perform a regressive array calculation with her new spreadsheet program, it's the checklist-making committee that gets chewed out. So adding new features is a kind of blame insurance. You can't get fired for buying the program that does everything. And anyone who finds a program too difficult to use will never admit it anyway, because no one wants to appear dumber than everyone else.

So corporations demand features, and software companies do their best to add them. From the software company's point of view, this is not a problem. The manufacturers say, "If you don't need a feature, don't use it." Right. Just like you can decide not to use the power windows on a car.

Actually, all those unused features hang like cellulite around the core of the program. Word processors that once required only 256K of memory or one megabyte of storage on a hard disk now require two megabytes of memory, hog eight or ten megabytes of hard disk space, and slow down the computer.

Extra features also make a program harder to use. You have to hunt through a bunch of features you don't want in order to use the ones you really need. A menu may have twelve commands on it, but you use only three of them.

When you buy software, try to match the program's capabilities with your actual needs as closely as possible. Buy the simplest, least expensive programs you can get away with. They're invariably easier to learn, and they usually perform a lot better than some software Winnebago.

Standards Aren't Always Best

In each major category of business software, everyone recommends a couple of standard products. In word processors, the standards are WordPerfect and Microsoft Word. In spreadsheets, the standards are Lotus 1-2-3 and Microsoft Excel. But a program's status as the standard isn't always a good reason to buy it.

A program becomes a standard when it hits the market and is significantly better than the existing standard. People who spend their lives comparing programs — software reviewers, for example — recommend the new program because they like what it does. The sales momentum builds until everyone is buying the new program instead of the old one.

But once a standard is proclaimed, people buy it without even shopping around anymore. Tens of thousands of people buy the program, not because they've decided it's better but because everyone else tells them to.

You buy the standard program because you want the same program your friends and coworkers have. If you buy the standard, you can ask these people for help when you're in a jam. If you buy the standard, you won't have to worry about converting your files to another format when you share them with other people. If you buy the standard, you'll find lots of books and training programs for it. If this is your situation, then by all means, buy the standard. Run with the herd.

But if you work by yourself and seldom share files with other people, check out nonstandard programs as well. A less well-known program may offer more advanced features, and it will probably be less expensive. On the Macintosh, for example, the WriteNow word processor is a terrific program that costs about a fourth of Microsoft Word's price, and the Nisus word processor can produce text in other languages, even those that print right to left. On the PC side, Quattro Pro is a great spreadsheet that costs far less than 1-2-3 or Excel.

Dislodging a standard is like budging a glacier. Once the standard has been established, it tends to stay that way for a long time. We resist switching to a new and better product because that will mean having to translate file formats with everyone who still uses the standard. Any challenger must be so much better than the existing standard that switching to it is worth the hassle. Some really great products have come and gone because they couldn't buck the standard. Some standards have long overstayed their welcome because they are so difficult to dislodge from the top of the sales heap.

So just because a program is the standard, that doesn't automatically mean that you should buy it. You may have to dig around some even to get a chance to look at some of the non-standard products, since many retailers don't carry them, but the hunt can be worth it.

Shareware: No-Frills Software

Software comes in many enticing varieties, but we often don't explore different programs because of budget constraints. Most commercial programs cost between $50 and $500, so collecting programs can be an expensive proposition. The alternative to high software prices is shareware. Shareware is software that you get through a user group or by copying, or *downloading,* it from a commercial computer information service, such as Prodigy, CompuServe, and America OnLine.

Usually shareware comes as a couple of files on a disk rather than in some fancy package. You get a copy of the software and a separate file containing a manual. (You have to print the manual out yourself.) All you risk is the cost of the disk you copied the program onto, or the cost of the time you spent getting it from a computer information service.

If you like the program, you're often asked to send the author a very reasonable fee — usually less than $50, and often as little as $5 or $10. Some programs are free.

Along with low prices, shareware usually offers more variety than you'll find in commercial programs. You can often find handy little utility programs that you can't even buy from a store or catalog. Lots of great shareware programs could never make it commercially because the market for them isn't large enough. They're like the local cable TV program that covers city council meetings — not prime-time network material, but essential for some people.

Sometimes, shareware programs are better than anything available commercially; I can think of some virus-checking utilities and communications programs in particular. But shareware isn't without its drawbacks. First, it's more subjective. Commercial programs are hashed out by design committees and customer focus groups, so their look and behavior reflect a broad consensus. Shareware programs don't always act the way you think they should. They might have commands that have unusual names or appear in unusual places.

Second, the manuals are usually less helpful. Shareware manuals are often written by the program's author or a friend rather than by technical-writing pros. Commercial programs' manuals are often difficult to understand, but shareware manuals are generally even worse.

Finally, there's usually no technical support. Most commercial programs come with some phone-in technical support. Most shareware programs don't.

Despite these drawbacks, shareware is well worth looking into. Check out the shareware library at your local user group. Some books list names and brief descriptions of thousands of shareware programs. Remember, though, that if you end up using one of these programs, you should pay for it if the author asks for a fee.

Ask about Support

Most people need some sort of hand-holding as they learn to use a program, and you can't always rely on friends and co-workers to be there when you need them. Don't buy any commercial program whose manufacturer won't support it.

At a minimum, the manufacturer should have a phone line staffed by actual human beings who can take your questions and try to answer them. You should be able to reach these people without having to listen to some awful local radio station for an hour every time you call.

Some companies have better support than others. The size of the company has little to do with the quality of its support. Some tiny firms are terrific, and some giant companies are terrible. Salespeople will tell you what you want to hear about support, but friends and user group members will be much more candid. Ask around.

CHAPTER 4

Where Do You Put It?

The Computer Needs a Home

Many people buy a computer and take it home and just stick it somewhere like the kitchen table. I've seen computers on rickety TV trays, on chest-high countertops, on end tables, and even on the floor.

If you seriously plan to use your computer for real work, you'll have to do better than this. Before you take the new computer back to your home or office, plan a place for it that makes sense.

What makes sense?

A good surface. Set the system up on a sturdy surface that has enough room for the computer, monitor, keyboard, and mouse. You may want to put the computer itself on the floor under the surface. If you do, make sure it's on a stand or a piece of wood and not directly on a carpet; you can block important cooling vents if you put it on a carpet.

A good power source. The surface should be close to a

three-prong grounded electrical outlet. If you're not sure the outlet is grounded, have it checked. Using an ungrounded outlet can fry your computer if there's a power surge or outage.

Space. Allow at least four inches of space between the back of the computer and the wall or cabinet, so there's room for the cables that come out of the back of the computer. The surface should be wide enough for you to put the keyboard in front of the monitor and sit so your eyes are eighteen to twenty-eight inches away from the screen when you're typing.

Proper lighting. Set up the computer monitor so there aren't any bright light sources directly behind or in front of the screen, because these will make it harder to see. If you're putting the computer near a window, for example, set it up so the window is at your side, rather than in front of you or behind you, unless you plan to draw the curtains or blinds all the time.

A healthy environment. Don't put the computer in a busy room where you'll be constantly distracted by the television, stereo, washing machine, or other members of the family. Bedrooms and quiet dens are good. Also, don't put the computer too near a heater, air conditioner, or humidifier, because extremes of temperature and moisture are bad for it. Avoid other environmental hazards, such as dust, smoke, cat hair, sawdust, bug spray, motor oil, and so on. In general, if something's not good for you to breathe or drink, it's not good for the computer either.

In short, the computer should have an area of its own: a sturdy surface in a place where you can use it comfortably and where it will be comfortable. Don't assume that you'll figure out where to put things as you're unpacking the system. Plan ahead.

Unpacking and Setting Up

The adventure begins. You've got half-a-dozen boxes on the floor and it's like Christmas morning: you want to rip them open and start plugging stuff together right away to get that computer up and running. Packing material, manuals, warranty cards, and small plastic bags containing tiny parts that don't look important get tossed into the pile of recyclables as you lay hands on your new digital buddy.

At this point you might want to remember that you're not plugging in a lamp here. You're setting up what is arguably the most complicated electrical device you'll ever use. Take it seriously. Follow this procedure.

1. Unpack carefully. Take one box at a time and unpack it completely. Don't rush. Use a knife to cut the sealing tape, and try not to tear the flaps. Remove any Styrofoam spacers carefully without breaking them. Lift the component out of the box, set it on the floor, and remove the protective plastic bag it comes in. Remove any other packing materials, such as cardboard inserts in the floppy disk drives. Check the box for the manuals and small-parts bags and set anything you find next to the component. Do this with each component until you have all the hardware out and unpacked, with the manuals and extra parts next to it.

2. **Check each parts list.** Find the packing list or parts inventory sheet for each box; it's either a separate sheet or inside the setup manual for the component. Make sure you have every part you are supposed to have. If not, make a note of the missing piece for future reference. Check each part for physical damage (dents, cracks, bent plugs or pins on cables) and call the manufacturer or store about returning any damaged parts for replacement.

3. **Read all the setup instructions.** Read the setup manual for every hardware component before connecting any of them. This way, you'll know how things generally fit together.

4. **Start with the system unit.** Plug the monitor, mouse, and keyboard cables into the system unit, then plug the other end of each connection cable into the external device. With a printer, for example, you plug one end of the cable into the printer and the other into the system unit. On some devices,

like keyboards and mice, however, the cord is permanently attached, so you only need to plug the free end into the system unit.

Most of the connectors, or *ports,* for external components are on the back of the system unit and may be hard to reach once the unit is in its final working position, so try to plug things in before you move it into position.

5. Check all connections. Check all the connections carefully. Make sure you've plugged the cables into the right places. Macintosh ports are clearly labeled, but some PCs have mouse and modem ports that look identical. Check the setup manual for the computer or component to make sure.

6. Read the start-up instructions. Read the instructions for turning each component on, and make sure its power switch is in the off position until you're ready to start the computer.

7. Plug in and power up. Plug all the power cords into grounded electrical outlets. (You may need to buy a multi-outlet power strip from the hardware store to accommodate all the plugs. If so, get one with a fuse in it, or better yet, get a *surge protector* from your computer store — it's a multi-outlet power strip that protects your equipment against power surges.) Then turn on the monitor and the system unit. Wait a minute or so and watch the monitor to be sure it comes on. If all is well, the operating system's interface will appear on the monitor after a minute or so and the computer will stand idle, waiting for your command.

8. Save all packing materials. Carefully put any Styrofoam spacers and protective bags back into the boxes from whence they came, and save all the component boxes. You will need them if you ever have to mail a component away for repairs.

9. Fill out and mail warranty cards. You should have a warranty card for the system unit, monitor, every other component, and each software package you bought. Fill out each card and send it in. This validates your right to technical support and puts you on the company's mailing list so it can notify you of problems or upgrades.

10. Put manuals in a convenient place. Put all the manuals where you can get to them easily. Hardware manuals can go in a closet, because you won't need them very often, but keep the software manuals within arm's reach of your computer.

Don't Crowd It

Neatness tells us to put computer components as close together as possible. Reliability demands a little more space. Computers need air space between their components. They also need enough room for the cables coming out of the backs of the various boxes to lie in a natural position.

Heat is death to computer chips and electronic circuits. When you stick your printer up against your computer's main unit, you may be covering up some of the cooling vents built into the cases of these components. If the cooling vents are blocked, hot air is trapped inside the computer, disk drive, or printer. Hot air will shorten the component's life or cause unpleasant irregularities in its behavior, so leave an inch or two of space between each component.

You can put things too far apart, though. Maybe you've put your computer's system unit on the floor under your desk, for example. If it's so far from your keyboard and mouse that you have to stretch their cables to the limit to make everything fit, you may cause problems. Cables are made up of lots of smaller wires, and stretching them to their limit can break some of the wires, causing intermittent problems that are really frustrating and difficult to diagnose. Try to arrange components so the cables have a little slack in them.

This also means that you shouldn't shove your computer up against the back of a workstation or the wall. This tends to squash the cables coming out of the back and might also break some of the wires.

Don't stack papers on top of the monitor or use the computer and printer as a set of bookends, again because you may cover up some cooling vents. Another problem with piling stuff on or around a computer is that things have a way of falling over. Somehow, that unabridged dictionary you perched on top of your monitor falls off just when you're saving a crucial file to your hard disk. The vibration from its landing might *not* cause the hard disk to crash or make a disk-writing error, thereby destroying several hours' or days' work, but why take a chance?

A Desk Is Not a Workstation

Having spent hundreds or thousands of dollars on a computer system, most people give almost no thought to the furniture they put it on. You get the computer back home or to the office and, casting around for a place to put it, you think, *How about this desk right here?* There, you can worship at the computing shrine, your hands stretched over the keyboard, your head bowed toward the screen in supplication to the gods of cyberspace, as your omni-something CPU greedily shoves the telephone and stapler to the brink of the desktop.

Desktop computing, in the literal sense, seems like a good idea at first. You find a place for your computer right away, and you don't have to spend any extra money on furniture. The bad news is that desktop computing can ruin your life. Really. Desks are just too high.

As you type away on a too-high keyboard, your shoulders scrunch upward. Your elbows pinch in toward your body. Your elbow tendons strain to hold your forearms up, because the biceps, which should really be doing this, don't work when your hands are held parallel to the floor. You strain to see text on a monitor that's too close, too far away, too low, or too high. Your eyes bug out. Your face screws up. You get headaches, neck aches, backaches, and dizziness. You end up looking like a cross between the Hunchback of Notre Dame and a praying mantis.

These are the musculoskeletal facts of life in the computer age. "Desktop computing" has caused thousands of people neck and back strain, tendinitis, tenosynovitis, carpal tunnel syndrome, thoracic outlet syndrome, and other cumulative trauma disorders (CTDs) with equally impressive-sounding medical names. Some people have become permanently disabled.

Yes, all this can be yours by simply setting your computer on a desktop and trying to adjust your body to the computer, instead of the other way around. A little twinge in the forearm? No time to worry about it now — you're too busy being productive. Eventually, your body will force you to pay attention to it, but by then it may be too late.

A little time, money, and common sense spent adjusting the

computer system to your physical needs can mean years of safe and happy computing. So here's the scoop.

- Your keyboard's upper surface should be twenty-three to twenty-eight inches off the floor (depending on your height), at a level that allows you to type with your shoulders completely relaxed and your forearms perpendicular to your upper arms. Desktops are thirty inches high, which makes a keyboard sitting on one at least thirty-one inches off the floor. You can buy a keyboard drawer or an adjustable platform that screws to the underside of your desk so you can set the keyboard at the right level. Some computer tables have adjustable surfaces, too. You could also cut down the legs on an old table to make it lower.
- Your chair should be adjusted so your thighs slant slightly downward and your feet are flat on the floor. When the keyboard is too high, you may try to raise your chair to compensate. Usually, though, this means you end up on tiptoes. Typing on tiptoes strains your lower back, so if the keyboard is too high you should at least get a footrest. Of course, if the keyboard is at the right height to begin with, the chair seat should be low enough so you don't need a footrest, unless you're really short. If you are vertically challenged and you

can't lower the keyboard enough (no snickering here; I'm only sixty-seven inches high myself), get a footrest.

- The surface of your monitor's screen should be eighteen to twenty-eight inches from your eyes, depending on your vision. The screen should be at a level that allows you to sit up straight and look at the top half without bending your neck or back. With a computer on a desk, the screen is often too close and either too high or too low. Prop the monitor on some books to raise it, or get an adjustable monitor stand.
- If you can't situate your monitor to avoid glare from room lighting or windows, buy an antiglare screen for it.
- If you work at a computer for long periods and you begin to have vision problems, see an eye doctor about getting some "computer glasses" with a different prescription so you can see better.

Don't Strain

In the race between man and machine, the machine wins every time. The computer will happily continue to display stuff on its screen or accept input from its keyboard long after your neck petrifies or your hands go numb. Still, you can become so engrossed in what you're doing, or so pressured by some ridiculous deadline, that you plant yourself in front of the thing for hours. This is not healthy.

I've been using a computer for at least twenty hours a week for a dozen years. I've written more than twenty books and dozens of magazine articles. I've also acquired soreness in my fingertips and knuckles, tendinitis in my elbow, stiff shoulders, and probably arthritis, not to mention tripling the strength of my eyeglass prescription.

Some of this is just a matter of not being thirty anymore, but sitting for hours in the same position without a break hasn't helped. In the past year, I've been able to stabilize the deterioration by getting up and stretching every twenty minutes or half-hour. I used to think I'd never get anything done if I took breaks that often, but even a two-minute break and a good stretch works wonders on the old bod.

Any enlightened boss will let you stretch every so often, and it's really not as disruptive to your work as you might think. You'll always find the computer waiting patiently just where you left off when you come back.

CHAPTER 5

From Novice to Guru in Seven Easy Steps

When you're new to computing or to a program, there seems to be so much to learn — all those weird-sounding terms and procedures swirl around like so many gnats. But you can bring order to the chaos by proceeding a step at a time. Start with the most basic stuff and move ahead to more specific details as you become comfortable. Here's what to do.

1. Start with the Hardware

Some computer components aren't like anything else you've ever used. Others look like things you've used before, but they behave differently. The first thing to learn on your computer is how to work its keys, switches, and buttons. This may sound obvious, but people really have mistaken a mouse for a foot pedal, and people really have tried to send a fax with their computer by holding a piece of paper up against the monitor screen.

You can learn about your computer's hardware by taking a quick look at the manual that came with each component. Here's what you should know about each component in your computer system. (Remember, if you have a laptop or portable computer, many of these components come in one package.)

The System Unit

- Where's the power switch, and which position is on?
- Is there a key switch on the computer? Which position is unlocked? I've seen people sit helplessly in front of a system that wouldn't go on because the key switch was locked. Usually the key switch is next to the power switch.
- Does your PC have a turbo button that changes the processor's clock speed? If it does, find out which button position makes the computer run fastest. Try starting the PC with the turbo button set each way to see the difference. (Some games don't run properly in turbo mode.)
- Where's the reset button? This is a button that restarts the computer, which is the simplest way to start over when you run into problems you can't figure out (see Chapter 11). On Macs, this button is usually not labeled, so check the manual's index to find out about it.

Never insert or remove a floppy disk when the drive is in use, or shut off or restart the computer when any drive is in use. You'll damage the disk and probably the drive, too.

The Disk Drives

- How do you open, insert, and eject disks from floppy disk drives? Macintosh computers eject disks through software commands; you just select the disk icon and drag it to the Trash icon on the desktop. On a PC, you push an eject button on the drive itself.

- How do you know when a disk drive is in use? A drive is in use when it's reading or writing to a disk. PCs usually have a light on each disk drive to show that it's in use, but you often have to listen for the drive to tell this on a Mac.

The Monitor

- How do you turn it on, and how do you know it's on? The monitor can be on but still be black because the computer's software isn't displaying anything at the time, or the computer might be fine but you can't see anything because the monitor is turned off or its brightness control is turned all the way down.

- What adjustment controls are there, and where are they? Find the controls for brightness, contrast, tint, hue, horizontal and vertical hold, and horizontal and vertical size. Play with them a little to see what they do. Your monitor may not be adjusted perfectly, and you may be able to center the image or make it bigger or brighter by tweaking the right control.

The Keyboard

A computer keyboard has a lot more keys than your basic typewriter does. Find out what they do.

Typewriter-like keys are the main group of keys. They mimic typewriter functions, creating letters, numbers, symbols, tabs, or spaces as you press them.

Function keys, usually located in a row above the main group of typewriter-like keys, are labeled F1, F2, and so on. These perform specific functions or commands in certain application programs or in the operating system. Each operating system or application program manual will tell you what they do. Many application programs come with paper overlays that help you remember which commands these keys issue in that particular program.

Navigation keys, such as Page Up, Page Down, Home, End, ↑, ↓,

⬅, and ➡, move the cursor around the screen or scroll a window.

The *numeric keypad* looks like a ten-key calculator, and is usually to the right of the typewriter-like keys. These are *dual-mode keys:* either they produce numbers and arithmetic symbols when you press them, or they move the cursor around the screen, depending on whether or not you have the [Num Lock] key locked down (see below).

The [Num Lock], [Scroll Lock], and [Caps Lock] keys lock down with a click when you press them, and they usually have indicator lights in or above them that tell you when they're locked down. It's important to know which position each of these keys is in, because they change how other keys function. The [Caps Lock] key makes every letter you type appear as a capital, whether you're holding down the [Shift] key or not. (Unlike the [Shift] key, however, [Caps Lock] doesn't produce the upper symbols on the typewriter-like keys). [Num Lock] makes the numeric keypad's keys produce numbers and math symbols when you press them, rather than control the cursor or scroll a window. The [Scroll Lock] key doesn't do anything in most programs, so you can ignore it unless your program manual mentions it.

Command keys, such as [Alt], [Control], [⌘], [Break], [Print Screen], [Insert], [Delete], [Option], [Return], and [Esc], issue computer commands

If you hold down keys on a computer keyboard, the letter, symbol, number, or command issued by those keys will repeat automatically until you take the pressure off the keys. Usually you have to hold keys down for more than a second before they begin repeating.

when you press them or when you hold them down as you press letter keys. For example, pressing [Alt] and [F] at the same time usually displays the File menu in a Windows program; pressing [Esc] usually clears a dialog box from the screen.

Take a good look at your keyboard and learn where all the keys are. That way you won't have to hunt for them when a software manual or screen message tells you to push them. Try pressing a few keys (with the computer off) to get a feel for them, and for how much pressure you need to put on them.

The Mouse or Trackball

If your computer came with a mouse or trackball, notice whether it has one button or two, and try rolling it and clicking the button(s) a few times with the computer off to get the feel of them. Then turn the computer on and see how the screen pointer moves as you move the mouse or trackball. You should put the mouse on a fabric or foam pad so its roller ball can get a good grip; otherwise, the ball may slip and the pointer on the screen won't track smoothly with your movements.

The Printer

- How do you turn it on, and how do you know when it's ready to print? Laser printers often need to warm up for a minute or so before you can print with them; most printers have a ready or select light that tells when they are ready to go.

It's Okay to Be Stupid

Jerkophobia is one of the greatest impediments to computer mastery. You don't ask questions and learn because you don't want to appear stupid. Following Mark Twain's adage, you think it's better to keep your mouth shut and appear stupid than to open it and remove all doubt.

But as it is with the budding tuba player in the next apartment, a little knowledge can be worse than no knowledge at all. One of the biggest problems we have with computers is learning just enough to get into trouble but not enough to get out of it once we're there.

A little humility and ignorance is good for all of us. The only way the real computer gurus got there was by not being afraid to look a little stupid along the way.

- How do you load paper into your printer? Can it accept different kinds and sizes of paper? If so, does it need to be adjusted to do this? Some printers have separate paper trays or feed mechanisms for different paper types.
- How do you change the ribbon, ink, or toner cartridge in your printer? This is usually fairly simple, but you can end up with ink or toner all over if you don't know how to do it.

2. Learn the Operating System

Once you're comfortable with your computer's hardware, the next step is to learn your way around the operating system. As mentioned in Chapter 1, the operating system is the group of programs you use to control the computer's hardware, manage disks and files, run application programs, and perform other fundamental tasks.

The best way to learn an operating system (or any program, for that matter) is to take one task at a time, read about it, and then try it out until you're sure you understand it. Operating system manuals can be really long and boring, though, so here's a guide to some basic things you should focus on.

How to Start the Operating System

If you have a hard disk drive, this should happen automatically when you turn on the computer. If your computer doesn't have a hard disk, you'll have to insert a floppy disk containing the operating system files before you turn it on. Try turning the computer on, letting it start up, and watching the start-up process. Get used to the noises your computer makes and the messages it puts on the screen as it starts up, so you know what's normal.

What the Operating System Interface Looks Like

When the computer finishes starting up, you'll see the operating system's user interface: the DOS command prompt (C:\>), the DOS Shell, the Windows Program Manager, or the Macintosh Finder. Consider this your home base, the starting and ending point for every computer session. This is where you open programs, copy files, reorganize disks, format disks, and (on the Macintosh) shut the computer off. Learn what this screen looks like and how to tell when you're there.

Remember, the operating system is always running, but you can — and usually will — have an application program running at the same time. You need to learn how to tell whether you're working in a program or in the operating system — that is, which program is active — at any given time.

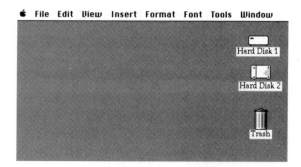

Here you see the disk icons on the Macintosh Finder's desktop, so it looks like the operating system is active. But in this example, the Microsoft Word application is currently active, not the Finder, because Word's menus are at the top of the screen.

How can you tell where you are? At the DOS command prompt, you see only the prompt with a blinking cursor. In DOS Shell, you see a window labeled MS-DOS Shell. In Windows, you see the Program Manager, File Manager, or Main window. Here are other signs:

Which menus are showing? You can tell you're in the Macintosh Finder because its menus aren't the same as the menus in any application. Learn the names of the Finder's menus and you'll always be able to tell whether or not you're in the Finder by looking at the menu bar. There are other ways to tell whether or not you're in the Finder (check your Macintosh manual) but noticing the menus is the simplest.

In Windows, the File Manager, Print Manager, and Program Manager windows all have their own menus. The window you're working in is the one that's active.

Which window is darkened? If you have several windows open at once, you can tell which window is active by noticing which one is darkened. In Windows, the active window (the window where your commands will take effect) is the one with the darkened title bar and the dark line around it. On the Macintosh, the darkened window is the one whose title bar and scroll bars are dark.

How to Control the Operating System

If you're using MS-DOS version 5 or later, try to use the DOS Shell to control the operating system. This shell is a half-step toward Windows: it displays major operating system commands on menus. It's not as simple to use as Windows, but it's a lot easier than having to learn DOS commands. You can use the DOS Shell by typing DOSSHELL at the DOS command prompt.

If you're using MS-DOS without the shell, you'll have to learn specific commands for each operation you want to perform, and you'll have to learn to type them exactly, because you'll get nasty messages like "Syntax Error" and "Abort, Retry, Ignore?" if you don't. Open your DOS manual (or a good DOS book) and read the sections about managing disks and files to learn these commands. Try each command to see how it works.

If you're using a Mac or Windows, you'll see windows, icons, and menus. To work with these interface elements,

- open a window by double-clicking on its icon.

- close a window by clicking (on a Mac) or double-clicking (in Windows) its close box.
- resize a window by dragging its size box (on a Mac) or its edges (in Windows).
- move a window by dragging it by its title bar.
- display a menu by pointing to the menu name and holding the mouse button down.
- choose a command by displaying a menu, holding down the mouse button, pointing to the command, and releasing the mouse button.
- use a dialog box. Choose a command with an ellipsis (…) after its name to display a dialog box, then try clicking to choose different options or typing information in the entry boxes. Don't click the OK button, though, unless you're sure you want to issue the command using the options you've chosen. Instead, click the Cancel button to put the dialog box away without making any changes when you've finished trying things out.

Poke around. Try each operation until you're comfortable with it. The computer won't blow up. Honest.

How to Tell One Disk Drive from Another

On a PC, each disk drive has a letter designation (A:, B:, C:, and so on). On a Mac, you name each disk yourself. On a PC, the A: and B: drives are usually floppy disk drives, and those labeled C: or higher are usually hard disks or CD-ROM drives. Find out which disk is which on your computer. Learn how to look at the contents of each disk and how to switch from viewing one disk's contents to viewing another.

How to Organize a Disk

Every disk starts out as one big storage space or directory, called the *root* or *main directory*. This is like a large file drawer. Usually, though, disks are broken up into subdirectories (called folders on the Mac) to organize groups of similar files or programs better. For example, the root directory on a PC's hard disk is labeled C:\, but different subdirectories on it might be labeled C:\DOS, C:\WINDOWS, and C:\MSWORD. The DOS subdirectory might contain only operating system files, while the MSWORD subdirectory might contain only the Microsoft Word program's files.

When items on your disk are divided into different subdirectories, you must know how to locate and open each subdirectory so you can find what you need, and you must know how to tell which subdirectory you're viewing at any time. The

DOS prompt shows the name of the currently open subdirectory, and the DOS Shell window also shows this. In Windows or on the Mac, you can sometimes display the contents of several directories at once. Learn how to tell which directory is open, how to move from one subdirectory to another, how to create or rename subdirectories, and how to copy or move files from one subdirectory to another.

How to Open and Quit Programs

Usually you can open a program by selecting it and choosing Open or Run from the File menu (in the DOS Shell, in Windows, or on the Mac) or by typing the program's name at the DOS command prompt. Once a program is open, you'll probably find a File menu at the left end of the menu bar, and the Quit or Exit command on it closes the program and returns you to the operating system. Try opening and quitting a program a couple of times so you'll know what the screen looks like when the program is running and when it isn't running.

How to Adjust the Operating System

Whether you use MS-DOS, Windows, or a Macintosh, there are several ways to adjust aspects of the operating system, such as how information is displayed on your screen, which disk drive and subdirectory are selected when the computer starts up, and how the computer's RAM is used by different programs.

If you're using MS-DOS or Windows, learn what the *AUTO-EXEC.BAT* and *CONFIG.SYS* files are, where they're located, and how to change them. These files contain commands that tell DOS or Windows specifically how to behave.

If you're using Windows, learn about the Program Manager, File Manager, Print Manager, and Control Panel programs.

If you're using a Macintosh, learn how to use control panel programs (or the Control Panel desk accessory, if you're using System 6), the Get Info command, and the About This Macintosh command.

3. Browse Through Your First Program

After — and only after — you've learned the basics of the operating system, fire up an application program. With any new application, the best way to get oriented is to give it the once-over.

Open each of the menus in your program and look at the commands on them to get an idea of where each command is. For example, file management commands (opening, closing, printing files) are usually on the File menu. Poking into each menu is like thumbing through a new book to see what the

Follow the Directions

Everyone wants to play the piano, but nobody wants to learn. The same goes for computers. We all want to be able to start up a program and begin using it immediately, but the shortest distance between ignorance and mastery is to follow the directions.

Most computers, operating systems, and programs come with a "getting started" manual or a basic tutorial that gets you going. These tutorials take anywhere from a few minutes to an hour or two, and they do two important things: they walk you through the main parts of the program so you get a general idea of what it can do and how it works, and they show the right way to do those basic things the first time, thereby saving you hours or days of messing around on your own.

The more willing you are to read the instructions, the less time you'll spend making mistakes and correcting yourself. Some mistakes — accidentally deleting a file or formatting a hard disk come to mind — can cost you hours, days, or weeks of work. A little time and patience spent to avoid them is well worth it.

chapter titles are and how long each chapter is — it gives you a sense of how the program is organized. You won't remember where every command is at first, but you'll be surprised how much you do remember.

One feature you'll want to locate right away is the program's built-in Help system. The Help system in most programs is a reference to instructions, like an electronic manual. Usually you can display the Help system's screens by pressing a function key or choosing a menu command. Find this system and learn how to locate specific information in it.

4. Learn to Manage Documents

After you've browsed through the program to get a general idea of where its commands are, learn to manage documents with it. These operations are pretty much the same with every application program, so you have to learn these procedures only with your first one.

The five basic tasks in any productivity program are entering data, editing data, formatting data, storing data on a disk, and printing data. You must have a document open on the screen to do any of these things, so let's start there.

Make a new document. Open a new, blank document by choosing the New command from the File menu. Once the document appears on the screen, choose the File menu's Close command and watch the document disappear.

Save a document. Open another new document (choose the New command again). Type some information into it (see

Chapters 7–9 for general information on how to type information into different kinds of programs), then press the ⌐Return⌐ key to make sure the data is stored in the document. Choose the File menu's Save command to save the document as a file on your disk. The computer will need to know the name and location of the file, so you'll see a dialog box where you can type this information, like this:

Study this dialog box carefully. It is similar in every application program — some of the options have different names or are in different places, but the basics are pretty much the same. You need to know

- how to tell which disk drive and which directory are selected. (In the example above, the drive and directory options are in the center of the dialog box.) After all, if you don't know where you're saving the file, you'll have a hard time finding it again, won't you?
- how to select a different disk or directory if you don't want to save the file in the current location.
- where to type the file's name and what sort of name you can use. DOS and Windows file names must contain eight characters or fewer and can't contain any spaces; Macintosh names can be up to thirty-two characters long and can contain spaces.

For this exercise, type *Test* in the File Name entry box. Before you click the OK button, notice which disk you're saving the file onto. Then watch that disk drive's light blink on your system unit as you click the Save button. You'll see the computer recording the file onto your disk.

Once you've saved the file, choose the Close command from the File menu to remove the document from the screen.

Open a file from your disk. Choose the Open command. You'll see a dialog box much like the Save command's dialog box, and it will list the files in the current disk directory. Your Test file should be listed there. (See? The computer really did save it after all.) Click the Open button to display it on the screen.

Save an existing file. With the Test file open on the screen, choose the Save command from the File menu. This time there's no dialog box, because the file already has a name and a place on your disk. (If you wanted to save the file with a different name or in a different place, you would use the Save As command on the File menu. This command would display the Save dialog box again.)

Print a document. Turn on your printer and choose the Print command from the File menu to print the file on paper. First you'll see a dialog box that lists options for how the document is to be printed. Study these options and change them if you like. Usually the standard settings are fine until you learn more about how the options work.

These are the basic operations you will perform with most of the documents you create, in any program you use. The specifics of entering information, working with it, and changing its appearance will depend on which kind of program you're using. But just by becoming familiar with managing documents and files, you're well into the computing comfort zone.

How to Choose and Use Books and Manuals

Somehow we have the idea that computers are supposed to do away with books. However, books are much more familiar to us than computers, so they can make learning easier.

But there are books and there are books. The manual that comes with a program is the software company's best effort to explain how that program works. It's the basic resource for learning the program. It may not be pretty and it may not be fun to read, but it usually contains what you need to know. Somewhere.

The trouble is that manuals are often organized for the convenience of the writer rather than the reader. They are written by people who know the program inside out. Often these people know the program so well that they assume you already know lots of things you don't know.

If you can't understand the manual, buy a book about the program from a computer or software store or catalog. Many of these books aren't as complete

5. Practice with Your Own Work

As soon as you're comfortable opening and saving documents, use the new program to handle a real-life project. Most programs have tutorials or sample files that introduce you to their features with a generic example, but you'll be a more attentive student if you learn with a project of your own.

as the program's manual, but often they're written for human beings instead of computer geniuses.

Of course, a book or a manual is useless if you don't read it, so don't just stick it on a shelf. Crack it open as soon as you install the program or set up the computer. Flip through it to get a sense of how it's organized. After that, look at a few specific sections to see how the material is presented. Each book and manual has a standard way of telling you how to type commands or follow instructions. Get familiar with the presentation method so it will be easy to follow when you look up information later.

Most programs come with a short "getting started" manual and a longer reference manual. Read the getting started manual first and learn the program's basics. Keep the reference manual handy and use it when you have a specific question. When a procedure seems more complicated than necessary, check the manual for a better way. You'll usually find one.

As you type that letter or prepare that budget or store those names and addresses, you'll want to change the way data is laid out or make changes to what you've typed. When you don't know how to do something, check the program's Help system or manual for the section that deals with that problem.

If you can't find a section that seems to have the right title, check the index. In many cases, you'll think of a command or procedure in one way (*typing,* for example), but the program or manual's author may call it something else (like *entering data*).

6. Be Patient

Every year, thousands of people try to see all the exhibits in the Metropolitan Museum in New York or the Louvre in Paris in one afternoon. The typical experience is one of diminishing returns. You can focus on things pretty well for the first hour or so, but eventually you're just cruising through the galleries, glancing left and right and wearing out your feet for nothing. The human brain can take in only so much at one time. This also applies to learning about computers.

It's possible to learn some of the very simplest programs in one sitting, but most programs are more complex than that. You should learn any program that takes more than a couple of hours to master in one-hour or half-hour chunks. Again, spend your early sessions learning the basic functions and save the refinements for later.

You're much better off learning a little bit of a program really well than you are rocketing through a lot of it so nothing sticks. It's like painting: if you only have an hour, it's better to paint one wall really well than to paint a whole room badly.

7. Expect Problems

Computing is complicated. With zillions of electrons coursing through millions of switches under the control of millions of programming instructions every second, something is bound to go wrong. Problems are normal.

Every problem interrupts our mad dash toward productivity. We just want to get on with printing that report or calculating that budget, and here's this problem interfering. It's not fair.

But problems are part of the deal. Watch an experienced computer user closely, especially when he or she is doing something unfamiliar. You'll see lots of miscues, false starts, and backtracking. The only difference between you and the gurus is that the gurus don't tear their hair, panic, or get righteously indignant every time something doesn't go right. Computer gurus take problems in stride, so much so that overcoming problems seems part of their normal work. And that's because it is. The sooner you accept problems and miscues as part of the deal, the better.

CHAPTER 6

Averting Disaster

Don't Unplug or Move Anything While It's Running

This may seem obvious, but it's so important that it bears belaboring. Turn the whole computer system off before you unplug it or any of its components, and turn any individual components off before moving them. This goes for printers, monitors, external disk drives, modems, scanners, and anything else that's plugged directly into a power source.

Strictly speaking, the danger in moving something while it's running varies, depending on what you're moving. But rather than learning a dozen different rules for different components, it's far easier to remember the basic rule: just don't do it.

What sorts of things could happen? Oh, you could ruin a hard disk, gum up a laser printer, fry one or more of the chips on your computer's main circuit board, lose data, or corrupt files. Sure, it's a hassle to shut everything down when you move something. And you might get away with moving or unplugging some things some of the time without a problem. But why take the chance?

Keep It Clean

Computers may not seem to need cleaning, but they do. I've had three floppy disk drives die from dirt. Dirt or dust builds up on the disk drive heads, and eventually those dirty heads either ruin every disk they come into contact with or simply won't read or write data anymore. If you get a floppy disk cleaning kit and use it every couple of months, your floppy disk drives may last as long as you own the computer.

Monitors generate static electricity, which is a natural trap for dust particles. If you're a smoker, the screen will acquire a yellow-brown glaze in a remarkably short time. Try wiping your screen off with some glass cleaner once every few days — you'll be amazed at how much gunk is on it. If it has a mesh glare filter, take the filter off and use a lint-free cloth or a soft brush to get the dust out of it.

Keyboards can also get a little grungy. Dampen a cloth with spray cleaner and give those sticky keys a scrub now and then. (Leave the computer off when you do this, or you'll confuse it by pressing all those keys as you wipe them.)

Internal cleanliness is important, too. When you first get your computer, all that disk space seems endless. But disks can become cluttered and disorganized just like your house, your car, and the top drawer of your desk. Look through your hard disk every now and then and delete any files you no longer need. If there are files you can't bear to delete but don't use regularly, copy them to a floppy disk. That way, you'll have the files if you ever need them, but they won't be in your way every day. Think of it as housekeeping.

Keep It Simple

Computers are complicated enough without your making things worse. You bought your computer to do word processing, play games, or whatever, and you'll probably learn some new programs as you go along. This is fine. But stay away from the useless gimmicks.

Programs that randomly change the pattern of your desktop, emit flushing sounds when you eject a disk, or play "Hail to the Chief" when you start the computer each day are the software equivalent of fuzzy dice hanging from the rearview mirror of your car. These gimmicks may be cute, but they make your computer's real job harder. Each gimmick program uses up memory and processing power. Each draws the computer's attention away from the real work you're trying to do.

If this warning comes too late and your computer is doing all sorts of weird stuff, you probably have way too many gimmick programs running. These are usually small programs that load automatically when you start up your computer (they're called *memory-resident programs* or *TSRs* on PCs and *inits* or *extensions* on a Macintosh). Try removing a few of them and see if things get better.

Naturally, every software manufacturer thinks its little add-on is the greatest thing since Jack Kilby invented integrated circuits. Every little utility program promises to make your life so much better or more fun that you simply can't live without it. Individually, none of them seems so bad.

But reliability is more important than anything. Useless utility programs help diminish it. An occasional laugh or a tiny improvement won't mean much if it causes your system to crash just when you're rushing to get that annual report out.

Back Up Everything

If you use a computer long enough, you'll eventually lose a file or a whole disk. Sometimes the hard disk crashes. Sometimes the computer burps and messes up a particular file. Sometimes you ruin or delete a file by accident. Floppy disks in particular become unreadable after months or years. They wear out even if you never use them, because the magnetic coating degrades.

If you have a backup copy of a trashed file or disk, these things are a minor annoyance. If you don't, they're a major disaster.

You need three kinds of backups:

- copies of all your data files, which you update constantly as you change them;
- backup floppy disk copies of all your programs and system software installation disks; and
- a complete backup of your hard disk, made with a backup utility program.

This is important. You may think you're covered because you've got paper copies of your documents. You may think it won't happen to you, because your computer's new. You've got your original program and operating system installation disks, so they're your backup of those things. You can make it across Death Valley in August without a spare, just this once.

Well, you can make the backup now or you can pay the piper later. A backup now will cost you an hour or two and some blank floppy disks. A trashed disk or file later will cost you hours, days, or weeks as you try to recreate the files you've lost. Making backups isn't all that hard, anyway. Here are some suggestions.

- To back up your operating system and application programs, copy the original floppy disks and store the copies in a safe place away from your computer.
- To back up files you create or modify every day, keep a floppy disk or an extra hard disk available and save the file onto both your main hard disk and this extra disk several times a day.
- If files are crucial to your job or business, make a backup on a floppy disk or other portable storage device and take it home with you. (If the office burns down, you won't lose your data.)
- Once every week or month, depending on how much you change on your disk and how often, make a complete backup of your entire hard disk. This not only copies every file (including any you might have forgotten to copy manually) but preserves the directory or folder organization of your hard disk so you can recreate it easily if the disk dies.

Backups are essential. Period.

Save Early and Often

You can't save a file too frequently, but you can suffer greatly from saving too infrequently. For example, you might work for an hour on a new file and go off for coffee without saving it. While you're gone, the power goes out, the cat knocks the computer's plug out of the wall, or a coworker needs to use your computer and closes the file without saving it. Presto change-o! Your hour's work is gone forever.

Once you have named a file and saved it, it takes only a couple of keystrokes to save it again. So name new files and save them as soon as you begin storing information in them, then save frequently thereafter. Imagine how superior you'll feel when you calmly restart your computer after the next power outage, knowing that your files are safe.

Beware of Viruses

Computers do whatever programs tell them to do. A *virus* is a program that tells a computer to do bad things. Viruses are so named because they can copy themselves from one computer system to another and wreak havoc as they spread.

For example, a friend copies a file onto a floppy disk for you. If that friend's hard disk is infected with a virus, the virus copies itself to the floppy disk when your friend copies the file. When you put the floppy disk in your computer and copy the file to your own hard disk, the virus copies itself there as well. When you open that file, the virus goes to work.

Viruses cause all sorts of mischief, such as erasing files, damaging files, or simply creating random problems with opening, printing, copying, or displaying files. But they don't just appear spontaneously. Someone must originally place a virus on a disk on purpose. That virus can spread only as files or programs are copied from one disk to another.

Viruses were much bigger news a few years ago, when there were no adequate precautions in place to stop them. Software companies, corporations, and user groups that copied lots of programs or files on disks and networks didn't check for viruses, and a few became very widespread. Soon, however, virus-checking programs were invented. These programs look for and remove viruses from disks. Today, just about every organization that distributes software or has a large computer network uses such programs. Any new viruses are detected and stopped early on, so disks and networks are kept free of them.

If you're the only one who uses your computer and you don't exchange files with other people, your chances of getting a virus are pretty remote, just as your chances of getting the flu are pretty remote if you never interact with other people.

You shouldn't have to worry about disks you buy from a software company or user group, because these should have been checked for viruses before they got to you. But if you do swap floppy disks with others or exchange messages or files on a computer network, you should run a virus-checker regularly to make sure your computer hasn't caught one and to remove any that it has.

Be Prepared

The best way to get out of trouble quickly is to prepare for it. Here's what to keep handy in case of emergencies.

A start-up disk. Operating systems are really bloated these days, and most won't easily fit on a floppy disk, but if possible, make a floppy disk that you know you can use to start up the computer. You can usually make a start-up disk with a stripped-down version of your operating system; your manual will show you how. If something is wrong with the operating system on your hard disk and that prevents the computer from starting up, you won't be able to fix it — or access the files on your hard disk — unless you have a floppy disk that will start the computer.

A disk and file repair program. Buy a disk and file repair program, learn how to use it, and keep it handy. If nothing else, you can use it to recover files you've mistakenly deleted. You can also use it to fix some disk and file corruption problems. Most of these programs come with emergency start-up floppy disks that you can use when the hard disk is messed up.

Backup copies of your operating system, application programs, and data files. You'll need these in case the files on your hard disk become unreadable or damaged. Reinstalling the software is a fairly painless way to recover from a variety of annoying problems. (If your computer came with the operating system installed on the hard disk and you didn't get a set of floppy disks, get a set from the manufacturer, pronto.)

Don't Leave Files Open

Even if you leave your computer running all day long, don't leave files open any longer than you need them. Open files take up memory space you might better use for current projects. Also, an open file is susceptible to damage from electrical irregularities or human error. If you're finished with a file, close it.

Don't Work in a Thunderstorm

Power problems can be very bad for computers. An electrical surge can cause the chips to burn out, and a power failure or brownout can shut your system off just as it's writing a file to disk. If this happens, the file probably won't be written properly and will be lost forever.

If you have a choice in the matter, don't use your computer during a thunderstorm. If you must use it, buy a high-quality uninterruptible power supply, or *UPS*. A UPS is a battery system that kicks in automatically when the power goes off. These units usually include power-line conditioning, too, so your computer doesn't suffer from random voltage surges.

Even if you're not worried about power failures, get a surge protector to prevent increases in voltage from harming your computer. You may think you get the same power from an outlet every time you plug something in, but the level varies according to the overall demand for power in your area, the weather conditions, and whether or not the power company is working on your part of the electrical supply network. You don't normally notice these fluctuations because most household appliances are built to handle them. But computers are more sensitive to changes in power levels than other household items. A surge protector helps prevent too-high electrical levels from zapping your digital pal.

Finally, don't ignore your telephone line. Electrical surges can come over phone lines, too. If your computer has a modem, a power surge can come right through your modem into your computer. A lot of UPS units and some surge protectors also have jacks for telephone lines.

Don't Rush the Computer

Computers are amazingly speedy, and they can further boost your productivity by handling two or more jobs at once — say, printing one document while you're looking at another. But they can get confused, and when they do, the results are not pleasant. Give the computer time to respond to one command before you give it another.

It's easy to become impatient with a computer. That one-time racehorse suddenly seems like a glue-factory candidate as you wait an eternity for a file to open, save, reformat, or recalculate. You can get so impatient that you begin typing the next data entry or command before the current one has been processed.

Most of the time, the computer can handle your impatience. Most programs have *type-ahead buffers* that capture keystrokes or mouse clicks and save them until the computer is ready to handle them. But I've caused many a program to crash and lose some of my data by piling one command on top of another too quickly. Like the office go-fer who gets too many orders too quickly, the computer often forgets a few orders or simply gives up and goes on break.

Another good reason to do one thing at a time is that it will be easier for you to remember what you've done when something goes wrong. Most computer troubles involve user error, so a lot of troubleshooting involves retracing your steps to figure out what you did wrong. If you take too many steps at once, you won't remember what you did.

CHAPTER 7

Word-Processing Wisdom

Your Basic Word Processor

Word processing is by far the most popular application for personal computers. It is the easiest productivity application to understand, because it's a lot like using a typewriter. As we'll see, however, it isn't exactly like using a typewriter, and that causes problems for some people.

Let's look at some basic features of a word-processing program. (See illustration on page 124.)

In this example, the word processor's menus are in the menu bar at the top, and a document named CRITIC.WPS is open in a window below it.

The menu bar for this program, Microsoft Works for Windows, contains eight menus. Each menu contains a group of commands you use to work with the document.

The *tool bar* displays frequently used commands and menus. Here you see the font and style menus at the left and individual buttons that you can click with the mouse, either to execute

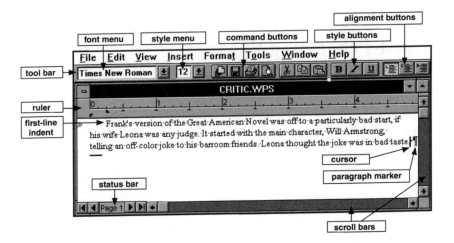

commands, such as print, cut, copy, or paste, or to choose various text style and alignment options. (This window has been narrowed to fit the page, so some tool-bar buttons are out of sight on the right.)

The *ruler* shows the width of each line in the document. You don't use the ruler to set the document's margins (the space between the edge of the paper and the text), as you would on a typewriter. Instead, you use it to set indents from the margins or the length of each line. To do this, you drag the black triangles from the left and right edges of the ruler.

To set and change margins, use the Format menu. You don't usually see all of the margin space when you're typing in a document, because you want to focus on the words you're typing, not on the space around them. However, most word-processing programs will show you the document complete with its margins and page edges in a preview, *or* page view, *mode, so you can see how the whole page will look when printed on paper.*

The left indent marker in the ruler is usually split into two parts. You drag the top part of the triangle to set a *first-line indent* — an indent that affects only the first line of each paragraph — as shown here.

The *status bar* at the bottom of the document window shows the number of the page you're viewing. Depending on the program, it may also show other kinds of information, such as the number of the line you're currently typing and the specific formatting options set for the text you're working on.

The *cursor,* or *insertion point,* is the place where text will appear when you type — it shows your current location in the document. In our example, it's at the end of the text. The cursor blinks so it's easy to find. Sometimes it's a blinking box rather than a line.

Word-processing programs come with tab stops preset every half-inch, but you can set them at other distances by choosing the kind of tab you want and then clicking below the point on the ruler where you want to set the tab stop. See "Use Different Tab Styles," p. 143, for more information.

The *paragraph marker,* also called a *return character,* next to the cursor indicates the end of a paragraph. Unlike what you would do with a typewriter, you don't have to press the Return key at the end of each line; the program automatically begins a new line when you run out of space on the current line, using a feature called *word wrap.* In fact, you shouldn't press the Return key at the end of each line. Press it only when you want to begin a new paragraph or add a blank line between one paragraph and another.

How Word Processing Works

Let's look at the basic functions of word processing.

Entering Text

When you open a new word-processing document, the inser-

The paragraph marker is an invisible character *that can be displayed on your screen but doesn't show when you print the document on paper. Other invisible characters help you identify tabs and spaces in your document. Word-processing programs usually have a command called Show Invisibles, Show Hidden Characters, Show All Characters, or Reveal Codes that you use to display or hide these invisible characters on your screen. Check your manual for more information.*

tion point is blinking at the left end of the first line. You type text into the document just as you would type it on a typewriter, except you don't have to insert paper and you don't have to press the [Return] key at the end of each line.

If you make a mistake as you're typing, press [←Backspace] or [Delete] on your keyboard to back up and erase the mistake. Then type in the correction.

Viewing Text

As you type, new lines of text follow one another and march toward the bottom of the document window. When there's no more room in the window, the lines at the top scroll upward and out of sight to make more room. To view lines that have scrolled up and out of the window, you click or drag in the scroll bar at the right edge of the window. (Most word processors also have a horizontal scroll bar at the bottom of the window, so you can scroll from left to right across a particularly wide document.)

To move the cursor, use your mouse to point where you want to go and click the mouse button, or press the navigation keys on your keyboard (see p. 88 in Chapter 5).

Selecting and Editing Text

There are several ways to change or edit text after you've typed it. Each method is appropriate in certain situations. The simplest way to change a few characters or one word is to move the cursor to the right of the word you want to change, press the ⌫Backspace or Delete key to back up over it, and type the ones you want.

Most of the time, however, you'll want to select a group of words, lines, or characters and change them. To select text,

1. Move the pointer to the beginning of the text you want to select.
2. Hold down the mouse button and drag the pointer across all the text you want selected.

3. Release the mouse button. The selected area of text is darkened or highlighted on your screen. This is the *selection*.

You can do several things to a selection.

- You can type replacement text. Whatever you type will replace the selection.
- You can remove the selection. To erase it permanently, press the ⌈Delete⌋ key.
- You can move the selection. If you simply want to move it to another place in the document, choose the Cut command from the program's Edit menu, move the cursor to the place where you want the text, and choose the Paste command from the program's Edit menu. The selection will be moved to the new location. (When you remove a selection, the text on either side of it closes up, or *reformats*, to fill in the empty space where the old text used to be.)
- You can paste in replacement text. If you have already placed another selection on the clipboard (text you cut from another place in your document, for example), you can choose the Paste command from the Edit menu to replace the current selection. For instance, if you previously copied *Fries* to the clipboard and you have *Burgers* selected in your doc-

Cutting, Copying, and Pasting

Cutting and *pasting* is the easiest way to remove or rearrange blocks of text in your document. First, select the words, sentences, or paragraphs you want to move or delete. Then remove the selection by choosing the Cut command from the Edit menu. Move the cursor to the place where you want the text, if you're moving the selection, and choose the Paste command from the Edit menu. The text you cut will appear in the new spot.

When you use the Cut command, the selection is removed from your document and placed in a temporary holding area in your computer's memory called the *clipboard*. The clipboard stores only one selection of text at a time. If you cut the word *Burger* from your document, that word is on the clipboard. But if you then cut the word *Fries* from your document, *Burger* is deleted from the clipboard and *Fries* takes its place.

To copy a selection instead of removing or cutting it from a document, choose the Copy command. The selection will remain in the document, but a copy of it will be placed on the clipboard.

Whatever you place on the clipboard remains there until you replace it with something else, even if you paste the clipboard's contents into your document. So, for example, if you wanted to insert the word *Burger* in several different places in your document, you could cut or copy it to the clipboard, move the cursor to the first location, choose the Paste command to paste it there, move the cursor again, choose Paste again, and so on.

ument, choosing the Paste command will replace *Burgers* with *Fries*.

Checking Spelling

Most word processors have a *spelling checker,* which inspects all the words in your document and matches them against a built-in dictionary file. When the spelling checker finds a word in your document that isn't in its dictionary, it displays a dialog box. You can use the dialog box to replace the suspect word with another one. (See "Spell-Checking Is Not Proofreading," on p. 134.)

Formatting text

After you've got the right words in your document, you can *format* them, or change their appearance. Some of the things you can change are

- the typeface, or *font.* Often you use a separate Font menu to select a different typeface.
- the text *style* — making it boldface, underlined, or italic, for example. Some programs have a separate Style menu with these options, or they may be on the Font or Format menu.
- the indentation, spacing, and alignment of lines.

- the location and kind of tab stops.
- the left, right, top, and bottom page margins.
- the number of columns in which text is arranged. Most documents have just one column, but many word-processing programs let you arrange text into two, three, or more columns, like a newspaper has.

See "What You Format Depends on Which Option You Choose," p. 135, for more information on these formatting options.

Previewing and Printing

When you've finished working with your document, you can look at it in preview or page view mode to see how it will look on paper, then print it out.

The software features wars have loaded up many word-processing programs with lots of features besides the ones mentioned here, but most of them are enhancements of what we've covered. The features discussed here are the ones most people use most of the time.

Edit First, Format Later

Word-processing programs can do lots of neat formatting stuff. You can center text automatically or make it boldface or italic at the touch of a key. Formatting is great, but all those goodies can really get in your way when you're first typing the text into a document.

There you are, in the middle of some fabulous train of thought, and suddenly you're wondering whether the first line of the paragraph is indented enough. By the time you play around with the indent, your train of thought has jumped the tracks and is lying in a weed-choked bog.

The words in a document are almost always more important than the way they look (except in advertisements). Focus on getting the right words down in the right order before you worry about things like indents and margins.

Another reason to perfect your prose before worrying about formatting is that the content sometimes dictates the format. For example, a two-word title above your latest poem might look great centered and boldfaced, but if you change the title to fifteen words on three separate lines, that look might not be right at all.

Ideally, you want to minimize the number of times you fiddle with formatting commands. Set up basic format options

> *You can usually arrange your word-processing program so each new document has preset options, or defaults, for the format you want. For example, if you like working with documents that are double-spaced and use one-and-a-half-inch left and right margins, you can set the program so all new documents have these options in place. If your program doesn't let you set default options like this, then open a new document, choose the format settings you want, and save the document with a name like Blank. After that, open the Blank document each time you start a new project, so the format settings are the way you want them. Then save the document with a different name, so you can store your work under that name and the Blank document will remain unchanged.*

when you first open a new document (line spacing, indents, and the font and size that's easiest for you to read) and leave them alone until you've finished typing and editing your text.

Spell-Checking Is Not Proofreading

Built-in spelling checkers are good at finding typos and misspellings, but spell-checking is not a substitute for proofreading your documents. These tools catch misspellings *(taht* instead of *that*), but they don't help when you've misused a correct word or when you've made a typo that results in a different but still correct word (*what* instead of *that*).

The only way to check for errors your spelling checker didn't catch is to proofread your document before you print it.

What You Format Depends on Which Option You Choose

When you're new to word processing, it's easy to get confused about how formatting works. Maybe you've typed a page of text and you want to change the lines from single-spaced to double-spaced. You choose the double-spacing command, but only one paragraph becomes double-spaced. What gives? Why don't the other paragraphs change?

Every word-processing program strives to give you as much control as possible over the look of your documents. In our example, the program changes the spacing in only one paragraph because line spacing is a paragraph formatting option. That is, it works only on the paragraph where the cursor is located, or on any paragraphs that are selected at the time. This way, you are able to choose different line spacings for different paragraphs.

Every word-processing program offers at least three different levels of formatting. Sometimes all these options are on one Format menu, but usually they're split up onto two or three menus. Check your program's menus to see where they are.

Character formatting is the most precise, since you can apply it to as little as one character or to as much as your whole document, depending on how much text you have selected at the time. Character formatting options include

- the kind of type, or the font.
- the type size. Type size is the height of a typical character, which is measured in points. Common type sizes are 10, 12, 14, and 18 points. (There are 72 points in an inch.)
- the type style, such as boldface, italic, and underlined.
- the type position, such as superscript or subscript. For example, exponential notation is usually superscript (higher than other characters), while numbers in chemical formulas are often subscript (lower than other characters).

To apply a character format, select the letters, words, or other portions of text you want to change and then choose a character format option. If you insert new letters or words within a section of text that has a particular format (boldface, say), the new letters will have the same format as the surround-

Word-processing programs always assume that you are creating new paragraphs one after another and that you want to carry an existing paragraph format over into each new one. For example, suppose the cursor is in the last paragraph of your document and you set that paragraph to double spacing. If you press the Return *key to begin a new paragraph, the new paragraph will be double-spaced as well.*

But changing the format in one paragraph does not change it in other existing paragraphs. For example, switching to double spacing in an existing paragraph won't change the line spacing in the previous paragraph or the following one. To change the format in any existing paragraph, you have to move the cursor to it or select it first.

ing ones. You can also apply a character format option before you begin typing, so the characters you type will have that format.

Paragraph formatting works on whole paragraphs. Its options include

- line spacing (single, double, or triple spaces between lines).
- alignment (whether lines in the paragraph are lined up on

the left or right margin, centered between both margins, or *justified,* which means aligned evenly on both left and right margins).

- tab stops (where tab stops appear, and what type of stop is in each location; see "Use Different Tab Styles," p. 143).
- indents, or how far each line is indented from the left and right margins.

Paragraph format options work either on the paragraph where the cursor is or on whichever paragraphs you have selected. If you select every paragraph in the document, then they will all be affected.

Document formatting applies to a whole document. These options include

- page margins, or the space between the edges of the paper you print on and the text you're printing.
- *page breaks,* which control how text in a document is divided onto pages during printing. Normally a word processor sets an automatic page break when the current page of text is full, but you can force a page break when a page isn't full by inserting a page break command.
- the number of columns. You can arrange text into two or more parallel columns running down each page.

- *Headers* or *footers,* which are lines that print inside the top or bottom margin on every page. These lines usually contain a document title, page number, author's name, or other identifying text.

In the more powerful word-processing programs, such as WordPerfect and Microsoft Word, you can apply document formatting options in areas called sections. By creating sections, you can use different document format options on different pages, or even on different parts of the same page. For example, you might divide a page into two sections so you can display text in two columns in the top half but in only one column in the bottom half.

To create a section, you insert a *section break,* which works like a page break except that it creates a new section instead of a new page. Check your program's manual to see if it lets you create and work with sections.

A Word Processor Doesn't Work Like a Typewriter

If you learned to type on a typewriter, you picked up certain habits that are unnecessary or inefficient when you use a word-processing program. Check the list below and see if you're still practicing any of these typewriter habits.

Don't put two spaces after periods. Your typing teacher probably told you to put two spaces after each period to separate the end of one sentence from the beginning of the next. But on a computer, two spaces after a period are too much — it usually looks as if something is missing. In fact, some spell-checking programs will mark double spaces after a period as an error.

Don't press the ⌨Return **key at the end of each line.** On a typewriter, you have to push the ⌨Return key (or slam the carriage return lever) to start a new line. Word-processing programs automatically start a new line when the line you're typing on is full.

Don't hit the ⌨Return key unless you want to start a new line before the current line is full. If you hit it more often than this, you'll make your document more difficult to format. Hitting the ⌨Return key inserts a paragraph marker, or return character, in your document. The program always starts a new line after each paragraph marker, no matter where it appears. So if you hit ⌨Return at the end of each line, you create a series of individual paragraphs one line long, like this:

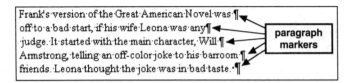

Frank's version of the Great American Novel was ¶
off to a bad start, if his wife Leona was any¶
judge. It started with the main character, Will ¶
Armstrong, telling an off-color joke to his barroom ¶
friends. Leona thought the joke was in bad taste. ¶

paragraph markers

If you later add more words to a line, that line will automatically wrap around, moving the paragraph marker to the middle of the next line, like this:

Frank's version of the Great American Novel was ¶
off to a particularly bad start, if his wife Leona
was any¶
judge. It started with the main character, Will ¶

Now you've got a line that ends where it's not supposed to. That paragraph marker after the word *any* has moved, and the program starts a new line after it. If you had laid off the Return key and simply let the program figure out the line endings, the lines wouldn't break awkwardly, no matter how much you edited them — the program would always adjust the line endings. The paragraph markers force the program to make new lines even when they don't look right.

Use first-line indents, not tabs. On a typewriter, you have to press the Tab key to indent the first line of a paragraph. Word-processing programs have first-line indent controls for this (see p. 125).

Once you set a first-line indent, the current paragraph will be affected, as will those you create immediately after it. If you use tabs, you'll have to remember to insert a tab each time you start a paragraph.

Use tabs, not spaces. If you really want to drive someone crazy, sit him down at your word processor and ask him to line up words or numbers in several columns by pressing the space-bar. It's better than Rubik's Cube — there's usually no solution at all.

Precisely aligned columns are no problem with the spacebar on a typewriter, because each character or space takes up the same space on a line. But on a computer, characters are proportionally spaced. An *m* is wider than an *i*, and an *m* in one font might be wider than an *m* in another font. Even blank spaces can have different widths.

When you want to align text or numbers precisely in columns, use tabs. Text always aligns exactly to a tab stop, no matter how wide or thin the characters are. Text aligned to a quarter-inch tab stop is always at one quarter inch, no matter what.

Use Different Tab Styles

On a typewriter, there's only one kind of tab stop. In a word-processing program, you can have left-aligned, right-aligned, centered, or decimal tab stops. Here's how and when to use these different styles.

- **Left tabs** are like the normal ones on typewriters. Text begins at the tab stop and proceeds to the right.
- **Right tabs** are backward. Text begins from the tab stop and marches to the left. These are great when you know where you want text to end rather than where you want it to begin. For example, if you want to line up part of a report name at the right margin of a document, set a right tab stop there. Then the name you type will start there and move to the left.
- **Centered tabs** are nice for aligning column labels directly above numbers or text in a column below them.
- **Decimal tabs** are the only way to align decimal numbers properly in a column when they contain different numbers of digits. The decimal place in the numbers always lines up on the tab stop. If a number doesn't have a decimal point, it's centered on the decimal tab stop.

Many word-processing programs also offer tab leaders, which are repeating dashes, periods, and other characters that fill the space between one tab stop and the next. Tab leaders are great when you have two widely separated columns of information. The leader helps the reader's eye follow across from a column on the left side of a page, like chapter titles, to a column at the right side of a page, like page numbers.

Avoid Format Overload

Anton Chekhov said that if there's a gun over the mantelpiece in Act I, it has to go off by the end of Act III. But just because your word-processing program has lots of formatting options, you don't have to use them all. When people first discover all those character and paragraph formatting options, many of them go a little overboard.

Here are a few rules of thumb to keep your document formats within the bounds of visual decency.

Don't use more than two fonts on a page. Newspapers and magazines rarely use more than two fonts on a page, and certainly no more than two fonts in one article. Designers often use a different font for headlines from the one they use for the body text of an article. So unless you're a trained professional, stick to two fonts — one for the heading or title and one for the body. And make sure the two fonts are visually compatible. If you're not sure they go together, stick with one font and just use a larger size or boldface style for the heading.

Use serif fonts for body text. Like the type you're reading now, a serif font has serifs — little heads, hands, feet, if you will — at the ends of the vertical lines in the *b, d, f, h, i, k, m,* and other characters. In contrast, sans-serif type doesn't have these serifs and seems to swim a little on the page when you read it. Serif fonts such as Times, Courier, Garamond, and Pica make blocks of text easier to read than sans-serif fonts such as Helvetica, Futura, and Univers. Sans-serif type often makes a nice contrast when used in headings, however.

Avoid fancy character formatting. Fancy character formatting — italic, underlined, or boldface styles or different fonts or sizes — is no substitute for clarity of expression. If your words don't convey the anger, frustration, or enthusiasm you want them to, don't expect formatting or punctuation to carry the load for you. Amateur writers often overuse quotation marks, exclamation points, capital letters, underlining, and boldface or italic type for emphasis instead of expressing themselves well. Their "documents" are littered with **punctuation** and <u>format</u> *crutches.* Any *emphasis* these **devices** was intended to add becomes *cheapened* with overuse until it's MEANINGLESS! When every sentence is "tarted up" this way, then *nothing* is emphasized!

Be careful with justified text. Many people think their documents look more professional if they use the justified alignment option in their word processors. After all, many magazines and newspapers use justified text for nice even margins on both sides of a column.

However, there's more to justified text than having all the lines in a document align evenly on both margins. Magazines and newspapers have professional layout people who use industrial-strength typesetting systems. These layout pros spend lots of time making tiny adjustments in the spaces between words and characters to achieve appropriate spacing on each line.

Word-processing programs don't give you enough control to make justified lines look right. A word processor simply varies the space between words to achieve the right line lengths. It doesn't give you any way to tinker manually with the amount of space between words or between characters. As a result, documents justified in word-processing programs often contain lines with too much or too little space between words.

It's much better to go with left-aligned text and have regular spacing between words than it is to have justified text   with   funky   word   spacing   like   this.

Look, Learn, and Apply

When using a typewriter, most people only have to worry about supplying the text in a readable format; real design work is left up to the pros. But word-processing programs give us many powerful formatting options. Everyone using a word processor can be a desktop publisher.

The trouble is, most of us aren't born designers. We can experiment on our own with different formatting options, but it might take a long time before we hit on the right combination. Fortunately, there's an easier way: copy designs you like.

Professional designers spend lots of time looking at other people's work and borrowing from it. Why not do the same? Collect pieces of work that are like the one you're doing — reports, newsletters, or whatever — pick out design elements you like in them, and then try similar elements yourself.

If your job is to put out the company newsletter, for example, look at other newsletters you like and think about how you can use some of the same design elements. Start with just one or two changes, like putting a shaded box under the title banner or adding larger capital letters at the beginnings of articles.

Think about your layouts as works in progress. Rather than settling for the same old thing, try making small improvements in each document. Your documents will look better, and your readers will thank you.

Preview Before You Print

Nothing wastes more paper than printing a document before you've really gone over it. You finish editing your text, slap on a few formatting options, and send it off to the printer. When you get the printout and take a look, you immediately start noticing things you need to change. Previewing your documents helps eliminate this problem.

Most word processors have a preview or page view mode that shows page breaks, margins, and sometimes the edges of each page. You can see exactly how everything will look on each printed page. With preview mode, you get a chance to see and fix problems you can't always catch when you're editing or formatting, such as

- *widows* and *orphans* (one or two words from a paragraph at the end of a page or the beginning of a new one).
- improper margins, first-line indents, and line spacing.
- ugly font combinations.
- improper heading alignment.

In some word-processing programs, you can even proofread your document one last time and make final edits before you print it.

Imported Documents Are Different

When you use your word processor to open an ASCII file or a document created with another word processor, you'll probably be surprised. (For more on file formats, see "Each Program Is an Island," in Chapter 3.) You expect to see nice even lines and paragraph endings, but sometimes you don't get them.

Imported ASCII files usually look strange because they have extra return characters in them. When a file is translated into ASCII format, a return character is often added to the end of each line. If the lines in the ASCII file are longer than they normally are in your word processor, they will wrap around in the document on your screen and the format will be all screwed up.

Documents imported from another word processor's native format sometimes have garbage characters, weird little boxes or symbols in certain places instead of text. These are usually markers that indicate formatting commands in the document's original program but that are Greek to the program you're using.

Don't despair. You can use your word processor to straighten out a crazy document quickly. First, if your document has gaps in lines or its lines end in odd places, it has extra return characters in it. Display these invisible characters if they're not showing already. Every program has a command to display invisible or hidden characters, so check your program's manual or on-line Help feature for instructions. Then delete the unwanted characters. As you delete unwanted return characters, the lines come back together as they should, and the gaps in the text will disappear.

CHAPTER 8

Spreadsheet Savvy

What Spreadsheets Do

Paper spreadsheets have been used for decades by accountants, financial planners, and others who want to display numbers and make calculations in rows and columns. In a sales forecast, for example, each column might represent one quarter's activity, and each row might list a different product. At the bottom of each column, the total sales for the quarter can be calculated.

Spreadsheet programs are used the same way, except they can store *formulas* that make calculations automatically. Let's have a look.

When you open a new document with a spreadsheet program, it looks something like the example on page 152. The document is divided into rows (labeled 1, 2, 3, and so on) and columns (labeled A, B, C, and so on). The intersection of each row and column is a box called a *cell*. Each cell stores a number, label, or calculation formula. Each cell is known by address box • selected cell • entry bar

| File | Edit | View | Insert | Format | Tools | Window | Help |

B2 · 750

Q1BUDGET.WKS

	A	B	C	D	E
1		January	February	March	
2	Rent	750	750	750	
3	Electric	125	110	98	
4	Gas	65	65	60	
5	Water	25	25	25	
6	Phone	110	120	125	
7	Insurance	0	0	175	
8					

its *address* — the row and column intersection where it is located.

To put data into a spreadsheet, you first choose, or *select,* the cell where you want the data to appear, then type a number or text and press Return or Enter to enter it. You can tell which cell is selected because a *selection outline* appears around it and the selected cell's address appears in the *address box.* (In the example above, cell B2 is selected.)

To select a cell, either point to it with the mouse and click the mouse button or press the navigation keys on your keyboard to move the selection outline. You can also select a group of cells by pointing to the first one, holding down the mouse button, and dragging the pointer across the other cells you want to select. A selected group of cells appears darker than the others. It can be very useful to work with cells in groups, as we'll see.

You can type numbers, a formula, a date, a time, or words into any spreadsheet cell. As you type, the numbers appear in the *entry bar* at the top of the document. In fact, whenever a single cell is selected, its contents also appear in the entry bar.

When you want to make a calculation, you type a formula into a cell. Once you enter a formula, the cell displays the formula's result. A formula might calculate specific numbers (*323 + 400*, for example), but usually it makes calculations using the contents of other cells. Here's an example.

B4	=B2+B3		
⊖			BUDGET.V
	A	**B**	**C**	**D**
1		January	February	March
2	Food	437.50	428.95	441.22
3	Rent	500.00	550.00	550.00
4	Total	937.50		

This spreadsheet shows rent and food expenses for three months. The selected cell, B4, contains a formula. The formula adds the contents of cells B2 and B3 together, and cell B4 displays the result of that calculation. (When you use cell addresses in a formula, they're called *cell references,* because the formula refers to those cells.)

You always type an equal sign, =, to begin a formula. This tells the program that you're starting a formula rather than just entering a number. After the equal sign, type the addresses of the cells whose data you want calculated, along with any arithmetic operators (+, −, *, or /) you need to make the calculation you want. (In a formula, you always indicate multiplication with an asterisk rather than an ×.)

Once you have entered a formula into a cell, the spreadsheet program calculates the result and displays it in that cell. Further, the stored formula recalculates whenever you change the contents of any cell to which the formula refers. In the example above, you could change the food or rent numbers in cells B2 and B3 whenever you liked, and the formula in cell B4 would automatically recalculate and display the new total.

Along with simple arithmetic operators, spreadsheet formu-

The specific notation that identifies a range of cells varies among spreadsheet programs. In our example, the notation is a colon, as in B2:B7. In another program, it might be two periods — B2..B7.

las often include named *functions* that make more complex calculations. Look at this example:

B8	=SUM(B2:B7)		
			BUDGET.V
	A	**B**	**C**	**D**
1		January	February	March
2	Food	437.50	428.95	441.22
3	Rent	500.00	550.00	550.00
4	Utilities	60.00	60.00	60.00
5	Insurance	101.60	101.60	101.60
6	Car Loan	175.35	175.35	175.35
7	Savings	125.00	125.00	125.00
8	Total	1399.45		

Here we want to add up six expense values to produce the total shown in cell B8. To calculate the total in cell B8, we could have used the formula =*B2+B3+B4+B5+B6+B7*, but that's a lot of typing to do. Instead, the formula in cell B8 contains the function SUM, which tells the program to add all the cells in the specified group, or *range* — in this case, cells B2 through B7. You can see the formula itself in the entry bar.

The SUM function is fairly simple, but spreadsheet programs have dozens of other functions that perform more complex calculations, including averages, loan payments, square roots, and logarithms. You can even use a function called IF, which examines the values in two different cells and makes logical decisions, such as calculating which value is greater.

Here's one more example:

E8		=AVG(B8:D8)		
□				BUDGET.WKS
	A	B	C	D	E
1		January	February	March	Averages
2	Food	437.50	428.95	441.22	435.89
3	Rent	500.00	550.00	550.00	533.33
4	Utilities	60.00	60.00	60.00	60.00
5	Insurance	101.60	101.60	101.60	101.60
6	Car Loan	175.35	175.35	175.35	175.35
7	Savings	125.00	125.00	125.00	125.00
8	Total	1399.45	1440.90	1453.17	1431.17

Here the totals for each month have been calculated (because formulas have been entered in cells C8 and D8), and a new column of formulas computes the average cost for each expense over the three-month period. Cell E8 is selected — you can see its formula in the entry bar. The formula tells the program to average the values in cells B8, C8, and D8. This is

> *Most people who use spreadsheets never get beyond using simple functions like SUM and AVG. This is like using an expensive stove just to boil water. Every spreadsheet program has at least fifty functions that can do zillions of incredible things. Do yourself a favor. Check the function reference in your spreadsheet manual or book to learn more about functions and what they can do.*

easier than manually computing the average with the formula $=(B8+C8+D8)/3$.

So spreadsheets let you arrange numbers and text in rows and columns, but most important, they can store formulas that make calculations quickly and easily.

Along with entering data and formulas, you can change the appearance, or formatting, of a spreadsheet document in various ways. You can

- make columns wider or narrower, to accommodate short or long numbers or labels better.
- change the font (typeface), size, or style of the text or numbers in your data. (In the examples above, some cells are boldfaced.)

- choose different display options for numbers. For example, you can display numbers in currency notation ($5.00) or plain notation (5.00, 5.0, or 5).
- align data at the left, center, or right edge of each cell.
- insert new, blank rows or columns between existing ones, or delete rows or columns you don't need.
- sort rows in alphabetical, chronological, or numerical order.

Most spreadsheet programs also let you make charts from your data. You can select a group of cells and then display their numbers in a bar, pie, or line chart, for example. The more powerful the spreadsheet program is, the more sophisticated your charting options are.

Faster Formulas with Copy and Paste

Even a small spreadsheet can contain a lot of formulas. For example, the budget on p. 156 contains ten different formulas that compute its monthly totals and three-month averages. But you don't have to type a formula into every cell in which you want a calculation result to appear; you can copy and paste formulas instead.

Let's assume that we've just entered the first formula to total the January expenses in a budget spreadsheet like this:

B8	=SUM(B2:B7)		
			BUDGET.V
	A	**B**	**C**	**D**
1		January	February	March
2	Food	437.50	428.95	441.22
3	Rent	500.00	550.00	550.00
4	Utilities	60.00	60.00	60.00
5	Insurance	101.60	101.60	101.60
6	Car Loan	175.35	175.35	175.35
7	Savings	125.00	125.00	125.00
8	Total	1399.45		

The basic calculation in cell B8 (adding up the contents of cells B2 through B7) is the same calculation we want to make in cells C8 and D8. In each place, we want the formula to add the contents of the six cells directly above it.

Rather than retyping the formula into cells C8 and D8, we can copy the one from cell B8. To do this,

1. Select cell B8.
2. Choose the Copy command from the Edit menu. This places a copy of cell B8's formula into the spreadsheet program's temporary memory space, or clipboard.
3. Select cell C8.
4. Choose the Paste command from the Edit menu. A copy of the formula appears in cell C8, like this:

C8		=SUM(C2:C7)	

			BUDGET.V
	A	**B**	**C**	**D**
1		January	February	March
2	Food	437.50	428.95	441.22
3	Rent	500.00	550.00	550.00
4	Utilities	60.00	60.00	60.00
5	Insurance	101.60	101.60	101.60
6	Car Loan	175.35	175.35	175.35
7	Savings	125.00	125.00	125.00
8	Total	1399.45	1440.90	

Notice that the cell references in this new formula aren't the same as in the formula we copied. In cell B8 the references are *B2:B7*, and in cell C8 the references are *C2:C7*. When we made the copy, the program automatically adjusted the cell references in the formula to its new location. If we now selected cell D8 and chose the Paste command again, the formula that appeared there would contain the references *D2:D7*.

The cell references adjust to match the location of a copied formula because they're *relative* cell references — that is, they are relative to the position of the formula in which they are originally entered. When you copy a formula that contains relative references, the references always adjust to the formula's new location.

Copying and pasting with relative references can make your

Spreadsheet programs assume that you want relative references in your formulas. You must specify a cell reference differently to indicate that the reference is not *relative. For example, instead of the relative reference B7, you might type B7. The dollar signs indicate that this is an* absolute cell reference, *which means that the reference doesn't change no matter where you copy or move the formula that contains it. The symbol that denotes an absolute reference can vary with the spreadsheet program you're using.*

spreadsheeting life a lot easier, and can help ensure the accuracy of your calculations. We'll see how later in this chapter.

Make a Plan

Before you jump into a new spreadsheet and start entering stuff like crazy, think about what you want the spreadsheet to accomplish and how you can best achieve your goal. Have a plan in mind before you start entering data.

It's like building a house. You shift walls and resize rooms on paper until you get a design that's easy to move around in, flows logically from one place to another, and makes the most efficient use of space. Your finished spreadsheet, or *model*, should be easy to use, easy to move around in, easy to read, and easy to print out.

The best plans start from a series of questions. For instance, suppose we're working on a budget spreadsheet that shows expenses over time. Essentially, you need to decide what information you want to include, and how you want it presented. You might ask yourself these questions:

- What are the different categories for your data? Do you want to list expenses for electricity, gas, and water in separate rows, or just lump them all into one row called Utilities?
- What time periods do you want to show? Are you showing expenses by the week, month, or year?
- Should you group all the expense categories into one block of rows with one total at the bottom, or should you break up the categories into smaller groups (*submodels*) with their own subtotals?
- If you know you'll want a chart of your data, have you broken up the data so you can make the chart you need? If you want to produce a chart of sales totals by quarters, for example, you won't be able to do that easily if your spreadsheet only lists sales figures by the month.
- Which layout makes the best use of space on the screen or

Your budget could lump all the expenses into one model with one row of totals at the bottom. Breaking the budget up into submodels such as housing, transportation, food, and entertainment, with subtotals for each area, will help you see how much each of these areas contributes to your total costs and how much each varies from month to month. If you make a separate submodel for household expenses, say, it'll be easier to see how that new lawnmower pushed you over budget last month.

paper? Should data be in columns or in rows? If you have a fifteen-month income projection that covers only five categories of income, for example, put the income categories in columns and list the monthly income in rows. This will give you a tall, narrow layout instead of a wide, flat layout that won't fit on one piece of paper.

It can be hard to visualize a spreadsheet layout in your head, so get out a pad of paper and sketch some different layouts. Be specific about naming rows and columns, grouping them into submodels, and arranging them.

If your spreadsheet is really large, try to put the most important and most used parts near the top of the document so you don't have to scroll to them every time you open the file. For example, if your group of household expenses changes frequently while your auto expenses don't, put the household group at the top of your document. Also, consider putting category labels in alphabetical order so it's easier to find a particular category.

Having a plan for each new spreadsheet saves you a lot of wrong turns and about-faces.

Substance First, Style Later

The whole point of making a spreadsheet is storing data and formulas accurately. So leave formatting choices like the size and style of type for later. The size of the type in your spreadsheet is far less important than the logic and accuracy of its calculations. Get the model working properly before you worry about whether the marketing vice president prefers Prestige Elite or Helvetica type.

Sometimes, of course, substance and style overlap. If your myopic boss grumbles when you don't use blank rows to separate parts of your spreadsheet, or when the columns aren't wide enough to leave some space between the data, then put in the blank rows or widen the columns before you start entering data and formulas. If your company's standard format is to alphabetize line items in a spreadsheet, enter the labels and sort them into the proper order before you enter values and formulas.

In most cases, though, you should concentrate on making the numbers work. The prettiest spreadsheet in the world is worse than useless if it presents the wrong conclusions.

Anticipate the Reader's Needs

When planning or building a spreadsheet model, pretend the reader knows nothing about the subject and try to anticipate questions he or she might have. Here are some specific things to consider.

List the title, date, and author. You wouldn't distribute a typed report in your company without a title, date, and author's name, so don't leave this information out of a spreadsheet. After all, a spreadsheet is just a report with numbers in it.

The title should explain the spreadsheet's purpose. "Budget" isn't very helpful. "Acme Manufacturing Income/Expense Projections as of April 1, 1995" is much better. You can put the title, date, and author information in a few rows at the top of the document itself, or include them in a header or footer that only appears when the document is printed on paper.

Make a table of contents. Most spreadsheets extend beyond

> *If your spreadsheet evolves and is printed several times over a period of days, weeks, or months, include the latest modification date in the header or footer. Sales projections made six months before a product launch aren't nearly as useful as those made six weeks after the launch. Your readers will want to know if your data reflects the most recent information.*

the boundaries of a single computer screen or printed piece of paper. A table of contents tells the reader what's where.

The simplest table of contents lists different groups of rows (or submodels) by name at the top of your spreadsheet, in the order in which they occur. If one submodel is to the right of another instead of below it, make the table of contents reflect that arrangement by placing that submodel's name to the right of the other's.

List your assumptions. If your spreadsheet's calculations rely on assumptions such as an interest rate, an inflation rate, a depreciation rate, or the projected cost of aluminum in August 1997, be sure to explain where these numbers came from and why you picked them instead of others.

List your basic assumptions at the top of your spreadsheet, right below the title and table of contents. If an assumption is specific to a particular section of your spreadsheet, say so. For example, if row 29 lists loan payments, you might add a note that says "7% Interest on Loan Payments in Row 29."

At times, a number in a particular cell needs further explanation. For example, if you list a miscellaneous income figure for July, readers may wonder whether you won the money playing Lotto or by selling the mineral rights underneath the employee parking lot. If a cell shows a figure for operating income, readers may need to know how you calculated it.

If your spreadsheet program lets you attach text notes to individual cells, use them to explain numbers or formulas. You can print the notes out at the end of your spreadsheet. If your spreadsheet doesn't have cell notes, then list the notes at the bottom of the model, referenced by cell addresses. An example would be "A34: Misc. income from sale of oil rights under southwest parking lot."

Avoid Typos

This is obvious, but it's important, because typos can have such a disastrous effect in a spreadsheet. The value of spreadsheets lies in their ability to reflect numbers and the relationships between them accurately. One little typing mistake can cause big problems.

> *If your spreadsheet has a Paste Function command, you can insert a function into a formula by choosing its name from a list. This way, you eliminate the possibility of typing the function name incorrectly.*

For example, suppose the formula in cell C9 is supposed to be *SUM(C3:C8)* to calculate a subtotal. In cell C23, the formula *C9+C14+C22* adds up three subtotals to produce a grand total. Now suppose you typed *C7* instead of *C8* when you entered the formula in cell C9, so it reads *SUM(C3:C7)*. Not only will the subtotal in cell C9 be wrong, but the total formula in cell C23 will also be wrong.

Because the numbers in one formula can rely on the accuracy of numbers in another formula, one typo can affect several calculations. The easiest way to prevent typos is to reduce the amount of typing you do. Here are some ideas about that.

Use functions whenever possible. Functions simplify your work. Instead of typing *A1+A2+A3+A4* to add the contents of four cells, type *SUM(A1:A4)*. Functions make formulas shorter, so they reduce the opportunities for typing mistakes.

Click on cells to insert their references. Typing is only one way to specify cell references in a formula. Once you select the cell where you want to enter a formula and you type an equal sign to begin it, you can click on any cell to add its reference to the formula. For example, to enter the formula =A3+A4, you could

1. Type = to begin the formula.
2. Point to cell A3 and click the mouse button. The spreadsheet adds *A3* to the formula.
3. Type +.
4. Point to cell A4 and click the mouse button. The spreadsheet adds *A4* to the formula, so it now reads =A3+A4.
5. Press [Return] or [Enter] to enter the formula.

In addition to clicking on individual cells, you can hold down the mouse button and drag the pointer to select any group of cells as you build a formula. When you select a group of cells this way, the references for that whole group will be added to the formula. For example, if you type = and then hold down the mouse button as you drag the pointer across cells A3, A4, and A5, the program will enter the reference *A3:A5* in the formula.

When you point to a cell, you know exactly which cell you're pointing to, so it's harder to enter the wrong cell reference. If you type cell references, though, a slip of the finger could have you including the July passive income figure in your May manufacturing expense totals.

Copy formulas. If you're using essentially the same formula in several different cells, copy the original formula and paste it into the other cells where you need it instead of typing it over and over. (See "Faster Formulas with Copy and Paste," p. 158.)

You can speed up copying even more by using the Fill Right and Fill Down commands. These commands copy a formula or value from one cell into several selected cells to the right or below it, all with just one operation. For example, suppose you have a total formula in cell A21 and you want to copy it into cells B21 through L21. Select cell A21, hold down the mouse button, and drag the pointer across cells B21 through L21 to select the whole group. Then choose the Fill Right command from the Edit menu. The program copies the formula in cell A21 into all the other selected cells.

For more information, consult your spreadsheet manual.

Audit Every Formula

Spreadsheets give a false sense of security. They look so orderly and official, the numbers must be right, right? Wrong. The numbers can be wrong, and the formulas that calculate them

To make the checking easier, build cross-tabulation formulas into your models. Cross-tabulations add up the same data in two different ways, and the totals should match. In an annual budget, for example, you can total expenses by month (column totals), and you can total each type of expense by year (row totals). If you add up the total expenses for all the months (adding all the column totals), you should come up with the same figure as you do when you add up the different kinds of expenses totaled by year (adding all the row totals).

can be wrong. Check every formula and value to make sure it's right.

You can check values that you've typed directly into a spreadsheet easily enough by matching them against their sources, but formulas are harder to verify. Remember, a spreadsheet displays values in its cells — even when a cell contains a formula, it displays the formula's result, not the formula itself. So when you look at a spreadsheet, you can't immediately tell whether a formula that's supposed to total up values from four other cells is actually doing that. To check any formula, you must

1. select the cell that contains the formula;
2. look in the entry bar to see the formula; and
3. check the cell references in the formula to make sure these are the cells whose data you want calculated.

The only way to be sure that each formula in your spreadsheet is correct is to perform these steps for each cell that contains a formula. If you don't do this and you've made a mistake somewhere, you could be living in a fool's paradise for months, thinking that a calculation is accurate when it isn't.

It's best to check every formula right after you enter it. Check early. Check often. Check until you're sick of checking, and then check some more.

Make the Most of Each Page

Building a spreadsheet and then trying to print it is a little like building a boat in your basement and then trying to get it out the door. You'll often have more data on your spreadsheet than you can fit on a page. There's no ultimate cure for this problem, but there are some things you can do.

Conserve column space. Keep columns as narrow as possible without running everything together. Don't use space-hogging formatting options, and keep your numbers short.

- If you're dealing with even dollar amounts and every reader will know this, leave your numbers formatted without dollar signs and decimal places. The dollars-and-cents format uses up four extra character spaces in each column (dollar sign, decimal point, and two decimal places).
- If all your figures are in millions, represent them as thousands (*1,440* instead of *1,440,000*) and make a note at the top of the spreadsheet that all figures are in thousands. (You see this in annual reports all the time.)
- Don't use column titles that are a lot wider than the data in the columns. For example, if you label a column *January* instead of *Jan* and the column contains three-digit numbers, the label makes the column four characters wider than necessary.

Minimize margins. Make sure your spreadsheet document is set to the smallest possible top, bottom, left, and right margins. On multipage printouts you'll probably want a header or footer that contains the page number, your name, the date, and other information, so leave room in the top or bottom margin for that. Otherwise, make sure you're printing as close to the edges of the paper as you can.

Print sideways. If your spreadsheet has more columns than rows, print it sideways. Every spreadsheet program has an option to print sideways on a page, so the widest part of your spreadsheet matches the widest part of the paper.

Use smaller type. Smaller type sizes can give you more space on a page, especially for columns. You can get more columns of data across a page when the numbers are this big than you can when they're this big. You don't want to give anybody eyestrain, but 9-point type is surprisingly readable, especially if you allow a little bit of space between columns.

Print at a reduced size. When you've tried all of these methods and you still have one more column or row than you can fit on the page, see if you can print the spreadsheet at a reduced size. Windows and Macintosh programs let you print at reduced sizes (or scaling percentages), which shrinks everything on the page proportionally.

Keep Charts Simple

Everybody loves charts. Just ask Ross Perot. But thanks to creeping competitive featuritis, spreadsheet programs these days have so many chart types and formatting possibilities that it's easy to make a really confusing mess. That's not what charts are for.

A good chart should spotlight relationships between numbers, making the relationships plainer than they are when you look at the numbers themselves. Charting is not a contest to see who can use the most features from their spreadsheet's war chest.

Every spreadsheet contains a few basic chart types, such as bar, line, and pie, that have been around almost as long as sales meetings. These basic types are still the best. I've never seen a three-dimensional area chart that wasn't harder to decipher than it was worth. Here are some basic suggestions for charting your data.

Don't do it all in one chart. Don't try to make too many points with one chart. Instead of showing unit costs, units per worker, overall costs, and profits in the same chart, use two charts. Compare overall costs with profits in one, and plot unit costs against units per worker in the other. It's much better to prepare two or three crystal-clear charts than to make one chart that you have to study for five minutes to figure out.

Give your chart a good title. The chart title should point out the conclusion being presented. If the chart shows that worker productivity is declining, say so in the title.

Use labels to identify numbers. Unless the numbers in the chart's axes, pie slices, bars, or lines are self-explanatory, use labels to explain clearly what sort of data you're charting. A set of numbers could be units, dollars, salami sandwiches, points of light — lots of things. A data series could be a month, a quarter, or a century. Make it clear what the numbers refer to.

Add extra text to emphasize key features. If you want to draw attention to a particular number, bar, or pie slice in a chart, add a label to it. Most spreadsheet programs let you label specific data points in a chart, but if yours doesn't, copy the chart to a drawing program and add the label there.

Preview Before You Print

If your spreadsheet has a preview feature, use it. It's really hard to spot page breaks in a spreadsheet; they're little dashed lines that look a lot like the little dotted lines that separate cells from one another. Previewing is the best way to make sure each page will show the rows and columns you have in mind. It also gives you a chance to make sure your top or bottom margin is big enough to contain a header or footer, if you've added one.

CHAPTER 9

Database Directives

What's a Database?

A database is a collection of facts, such as addresses, sales orders, or inventory records. A business card file, a telephone directory, and a cookbook are all databases, because they're all collections of facts, or *records*. In each case, the records are organized in a certain way (alphabetically or by main ingredient, for example), so it's easy to look up and find a particular one (an address or recipe).

In a computer database, you can store facts about your customers, sales, friends, recipes, CD collection, investments, or anything else. Once you've stored a bunch of records, you can locate, or *find*, or *select*, records easily, arrange them in many different ways, calculate information from them, and print them out in *reports*.

For example, suppose you set up a database file and stored name and address records for a thousand customers. Having done so, you could manipulate the information in many different ways. You could

- quickly find and display one customer's address on the screen;
- arrange, or *sort,* all the addresses by ZIP code;
- display only customer names and phone numbers so you could print out a simple telephone list, or display customer names and addresses so you could print mailing labels; or
- select only the records of customers with addresses in San Francisco and then print those out for a specific promotional mailing.

Database programs let you store and work with any kind of information, including dates, times, numbers, words, and in some cases even pictures or sounds. If there's a way to describe or record information, there's a way to store and manipulate that information in a database.

How Database Programs Work

Using a database program is all about storing information so you can have as much flexibility as possible when you work with it later. Databases offer this flexibility by allowing you to break up information into different categories, or *fields.* For example, a database of names and addresses might have fields like this:

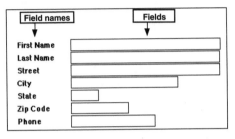

To store information, you type in one name, address, and phone number at a time. The field names tell you which information goes into which field. When you've filled these fields with one person's name, address, and phone number, the data is stored in the database file as a record. You can then display a new set of blank fields and enter another record.

Before you can store data, you must specify, or *define*, the fields into which you will separate it (see "Defining a Database File," p. 180). Once you've defined fields and stored information in them, you can

- sort or select records based on data in any of the fields (see "Managing Data," p. 187);
- arrange fields in different *forms* so you can view your data

on the screen in various ways (see "Arranging Data on Your Screen," p. 185); or

- arrange fields in different *report formats* so you can print them on paper (see "Creating Reports," p. 190).

Dividing information into fields, storing it, selecting and sorting the information you want to work with at a particular time, and arranging that information for display or printing are the basic operations in using a database. Let's look at these a little more closely.

Defining a Database File

To begin a new database file, you choose the New command from the program's File menu. Because the file doesn't contain any fields yet, the program displays either a blank screen where you type field names or a field-definition dialog box. Page 181 shows a field-definition dialog box from ClarisWorks.

To define a new field, you type the field's name in the Name box, click one of the buttons below to choose a *data type* for that field, and click the Create button. In this example, five fields have already been defined and are showing in the list, and a sixth field name, Zip, has been entered in the Name box.

Define Fields

Name	Type
First Name	Text
Last Name	Text
Street	Text
City	Text
State	Text

Name Zip

Type
- ⦿ Text ⌘1 ○ Time ⌘4
- ○ Number ⌘2 ○ Calculation ⌘5
- ○ Date ⌘3 ○ Summary ⌘6

[Create] [Options...]
[Delete] [Modify]
[Done]

The data type tells the database program what sort of data you'll be putting in the field, which determines how you'll be able to work with that data later on.

Text fields can contain letters, numbers, or dates, but the program treats all the data in them as text characters. Therefore, you can't make numeric calculations on data in a text field even if there are numbers in it.

Number fields can contain only numbers. Making a number-type field is a good way to ensure that nobody will accidentally type text into that field. When someone tries to type letters into a number field, the program displays an error message. You define a field as numeric when you want to be able to make calculations with the numbers it will contain.

Date and time fields accept data only in specific date (MM/YY/DD) or time (HH:MM:SS) formats. You define fields as date or time when you want to be able to sort in chronological order or make date or time calculations.

In the example above, all the fields are set up to contain text, so we could sort the database on any of these fields in alphabetical order.

You use **calculation** and **summary** field types when you want to make calculations with your data. These field types contain calculation formulas and display the results of their calculations. For instance, here's a record in an inventory file:

Item	Large Widget
Quantity	357
Unit Price	$1.05
Cost	$374.85

The Cost field here is a calculation field. It contains a formula that multiplies the Quantity field's data by the Unit Price field's data and displays the result. To define such a field, you must specify that it's a calculation-type field and enter a formula for it to follow in making its calculations. When you de-

Choose the Right Data Type for Each Field

Before you define fields, learn what different data types are available in the program you're using and decide which one is best for each field you define. The simplest programs allow only text and number fields; more sophisticated programs allow date, time, picture, and sound fields as well.

Whatever the selection, there's always a best data type for each field, because the data type affects how you will be able to manipulate the data later. For instance, it might seem reasonable to define a Zip Code field as numeric because it contains numbers. But in a number field, the database program will round off any number to its significant digits. In a numeric Zip Code field, this would mean that all the codes beginning with 0 would be rounded off to four-digit numbers. So much for sending mail to people living in New England. Knowing this, you would define a Zip Code field as a text field, so the program would retain the leading zeroes in the codes.

You can change field data types or sizes later on if you make a mistake, but it's a lot easier to get them right the first time.

fine a calculation field, the program displays a dialog box in which you enter that field's formula. The formula in the Cost field here is *Quantity*Price.*

Once you define a calculation field, the program makes the calculation automatically in every record. In this example, each record will contain information about a different inventory item, and the Cost field in each will show the total cost for that particular item.

A summary field also contains a formula, but instead of calculating information within each record, it calculates information from a group of records. Summary fields are mostly used for reports. For example, if we wanted to show the total cost of our entire inventory in a report, we could define a summary field called Total Cost and then create a report that contains it. When printed, such a report might look like this:

Item	Quantity	Unit Price	Cost
Standard Gizmo	88	$1.02	$89.76
Deluxe Gizmo	115	$1.23	$141.45
Large Widget	357	$1.05	$374.85
Medium Widget	445	$0.90	$400.50
Small Widget	1230	$0.72	$885.60
		Total Cost	$1892.16

summary field ⟶

In this case, the summary field (Total Cost) computes the formula *SUM(Cost)*, which tells it to add up all the values in the Cost field and display the result.

Defining database fields properly is essential to gaining maximum flexibility when you later manage or calculate in-

Break Up Information

Database files break up information into field-sized chunks. Generally, the more chunks you create, the more options you'll have for working with your data.

For example, in an address file, it may seem easiest to create one Name field that will contain both first and last names. If you do this, however, you won't be able to sort the file by last names, unless you enter last names first. Every database sorts by the first character in a field, so if the first character in your Name field is the beginning of someone's first name, then you'll be able to sort only by first names.

As you gain experience with databases, you'll get better at knowing how to break up information. Generally, it's better to go overboard in breaking it up than to put too much information into one field.

formation. Even if you don't get all the field definitions right when you first set up the file, you can usually add or remove fields or change their definitions later to give yourself more control over your data.

Arranging Data on Your Screen

When you begin entering data into a new database file, all the fields you defined will automatically appear on the screen in a *form* or *layout*. You use forms or layouts to enter data or to view it on the screen. Each field name is followed by a space where you can enter data.

However, most database programs let you create two or more different data entry forms, so you can view your data in different ways on the screen. For example, one form might show one record at a time, like this:

First Name	Bob
Last Name	Jones
Street	123 Willow Way
City	Carmiston
State	CA
Zip	91034
Phone	805-555-1123

Another layout might show records in a list, like this:

First Name	Last Name	Street	City	State	Zip	Phone
Bob	Jones	123 Willow Way	Carmiston	CA	91034	805-555-1123
Art	Silver	111 Colton Dr.	Willis	AZ	80034	602-555-0078
Fred	Woo	33 Trails Dr.	Chilino	NY	80053	702-555-5552
Maria	Gonzalez	43 Yucca Lane	San Lucas	AZ	80540	602-555-1223

If your database allows you to create several different forms for your data, you can give each form its own name. Each form can have a different group of fields in a different arrangement — you don't have to include every field in the file on every form. Once you've set up different forms, you can choose the one you want to view at any time by selecting its name from a menu.

Besides deciding which fields to include in a form and how to arrange them, you can choose various formatting options to control the way each field and its data appear. These options include

- the field size (how wide or tall it is);
- the kind of type, or *font,* used to display the data;
- the type size;
- the type style (boldface or italic, for example);
- the data alignment (centered, left aligned, or right aligned); and
- special notations, like currency for dollar amounts or different date or time formats.

Managing Data

If you've stored hundreds or thousands of records in your database file, you can't see them all at once on your screen, so you use the database to *find,* or *select,* the specific records you want to view at any time. You can also *sort* records in a particular order.

Selecting records. To select one or more records stored in your file, use a Find or Query command to tell the database to display all the records that match certain criteria. When you choose the command, you see a set of empty fields on a *query screen*. You type data into one or more of the fields, then choose a command to tell the database to locate all the records that have the same information in those fields.

For instance, to select the address records for people in San Francisco, you would type *San Francisco* in the City field on the query screen, like this:

First Name	
Last Name	
Street	
City	San Francisco
State	
Zip Code	
Phone	

Then you would click a Find or Query button to complete the query. The database will find all the records that have San Francisco in their City field. To find a record for Harry Jones, you would type *Harry* in the First Name field and *Jones* in the Last Name field on the query screen.

Sorting records. Sorting records is arranging them in a certain order, based on the contents of one or more fields. Usually a Sort command displays a dialog box, where you choose the field or fields on which you want to base the sort, like this:

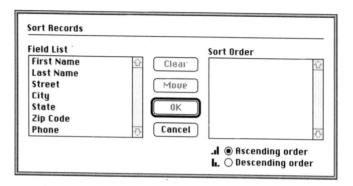

This Sort Records dialog box shows the fields in an address file. To sort the file alphabetically by last name, you would

1. select the Last Name field in the Field List at the left;
2. click the Move button to move that field name to the Sort Order list at the right; and
3. click the OK button to sort the file.

In this example, the Sort command's dialog box also lets you decide whether you want records sorted in ascending (A-Z) or descending (Z-A) order.

Most database programs let you sort on more than one field. For example, you could choose the Last Name field as the first sort criterion and the First Name field as the second. This way, if you had records for people named Reginald Jones and Karen Jones, Karen Jones would be displayed first and Reginald Jones second.

Creating Reports

To print your data on paper, you create a *report format.* Creating a report format is like creating a form or a layout — you name the report, choose the fields you want it to include, and arrange them. The difference is that report formats don't show the data in your file — they show only field names. Also, report formats include elements like headers and footers, which aren't included in layouts.

Here's a report format that will print a list of names and phone numbers in columns:

Header	Last Name	First Name	Phone
Body	Last Name	First Name	Phone

This report format contains a header (where the column labels appear) and a body (with the fields whose data will appear in the report). The labels in the header will appear at the top of each printed page, and the fields in the body will be repeated in rows down the page, one row for each record.

As with screen layouts, you can create different report formats to arrange fields in different ways. Another report format might arrange name and address fields for labels, like this:

First Name	Last Name	
Street		
City	State	Zip

Before printing a report, you can sort or select records. For example, you might have a report in which you have arranged fields to print addresses on mailing labels. Before printing this report, you could select only the addresses in California and sort them by Zip Code.

On page 184, a page from a printed inventory report shows the items in stock listed in rows and columns. The records are sorted by item number, and the report includes a summary calculation field that shows the total value of the inventory. The report format used to produce this page looks like this:

Header	**Item**	**Quantity**	**Unit Price**	**Cost**
Body	Item	Quantity	Unit Price	Cost
Grand Summary			**Total Cost**	Total Cost

The format contains a header (for the column labels), a body (for the rows of inventory item records), and a grand summary area that contains the summary field and the Total Cost label.

By selecting, sorting, and arranging your data in different ways, you can produce a wide variety of different reports.

Consistency Is Everything

A database file breaks up information into lots of different categories, but the categories won't do you any good if you don't use them consistently and make sure the data in them is accurate. To a database, a first name isn't a first name because it's *Tom* or *Linda,* but because it's in the First Name field. If you put Tom's first name in the Street field of a database file, you won't be able to find his record when you search the database for records in which the First Name field contains *Tom.*

You also have to be careful about typos. If you type *New Yerk* in the City field of one address record by mistake, that record won't be included when you select all the records whose City field contains *New York.*

It's easy to make a keystroke error that will later make it very difficult to locate a record. The record won't be found when you query the database, you won't notice that it's missing from the group of records that are selected by the query, and you won't know what error you made that has caused it to be excluded from the selection, so you won't know where to look for it. In a small database file, you can display every record and simply look for the one you want, but when you're working with hundreds or thousands of records, this becomes tedious, if not impossible.

To minimize errors like this, you can use field attributes.

Field types. If you know a field must contain a date, then define that field as a date field. That way, it won't accept nondate information if someone tries to enter it by mistake.

Standard or default values. In all but the simplest database programs, you can also specify *standard*, or *default*, *values* that eliminate the need to type data into certain fields. These values either appear automatically in each new record or appear on a list so you can simply choose the one you want to enter without typing it.

To define standard values, you first choose the field in which you want the values to be presented as options, then define the options you want to appear. For example, here's a dialog box from ClarisWorks that allows you to specify different types of standard values:

```
┌─────────────────────────────────────────────────────┐
│ Entry Options for Text Field "State"                  │
│ ┌─Auto Entry──────────────┐ ┌─Verification─────────┐ │
│ │ ◉ No auto entry          │ │ Verify field value is:│ │
│ │ ○ Data      [_____]  │ │                       │ │
│ │ ○ Variable  [Creator Name ▼] │ □ Not empty         │ │
│ │                          │ │ □ Unique              │ │
│ │ ○ Serial number          │ │ □ Range               │ │
│ │   next value  [_____] │ │   from   [_____]  │ │
│ │   increment   [_____] │ │   to     [_____]  │ │
│ └──────────────────────────┘ └───────────────────────┘ │
│ ┌─Input List──────────────┐                            │
│ │ □ Pre-defined list  [Edit List...] │                 │
│ │   □ Only values from list │  [Cancel]  [  OK  ]      │
│ └──────────────────────────┘                            │
└─────────────────────────────────────────────────────┘
```

The options here let you tell the program to enter or control which data is entered in a field automatically. To use them, you first select the field name in the field-definition box (see p. 181), and then click the Options button to display this box. (In the above example, the State field was selected, so any options we choose here will apply to that field.)

The Auto Entry options tell the program to put a specific piece of data in the field automatically. For example, if all your customers were in Illinois, you could use this option on the State field in your file. You would

1. select the State field from the list in the field-definition dialog box;

2. click the Options button to display the dialog box above;
3. click the Data button and type *IL* in the entry box at the right; and
4. click the OK button.

After this, *IL* will appear in the State field of each new record. This saves you from having to type *IL* for each new record and eliminates the possibility of introducing typos in that field.

Look at the other Auto Entry options. The Variable option tells the program to enter the current date, time, or other information in the field. The Serial Number option tells it to number records in order. For example, an Order Number field might contain *0001* in the first record of a file, *0002* in the second record, and so on.

Instead of having the program automatically enter a certain piece of information, you can also create a pop-up list that appears when the field is selected on the data entry form. This way, you can choose the correct entry from the list and enter it that way instead of typing it. You see this option at the bottom of the dialog box on p. 194.

For example, suppose you do business primarily on the West Coast and you want to define a pop-up list for the State field that contains *WA, OR,* and *CA.* This way, data entry operators can simply choose the right state for each record they enter. To do this, you would

1. select the State field in the field-definition dialog box (see p. 181);
2. click the Options button to display the dialog box on p. 194;
3. click the Pre-Defined List checkbox at the lower left corner of the dialog box (a blank list will appear);
4. type *CA, OR,* and *WA* into the blank list; and
5. click the OK button in the dialog box to complete the list.

Now the list containing the three state codes will appear whenever the State field is selected on the data entry form. To enter a particular state code, users can simply double-click on it.

Also, notice that the Only Values from List option allows you to determine whether the entry options for this field are limited to the choices on the list you've created or an alternative can by typed in by hand.

Data validation or verification. These options let you restrict what can be entered in a field, to ensure that the field isn't left blank or that it contains a unique value (one different from the value in that field in any other record) or a value that falls within a certain numeric range. If all the part numbers in your inventory are four-digit numbers, for example, you could set up a Part Number field so it won't accept any numbers that are longer or shorter than that. You can see these options at the right side of the dialog box on p. 194.

The simplest database programs don't offer many auto entry or data validation options, but if your database program does, learn about them and use them. You'll need all the help you can get to keep your data consistent and accurate.

Start Out Simple

As with any software, choosing a database involves a tradeoff between power and ease of use. But for databases, the power-ease spectrum is much wider than it is for other programs. It can take weeks or months to figure out some database programs, whereas others are simple enough to learn in an hour or so. Some require you to understand a programming language, but others can be managed with a few mouse clicks.

It's best to start out with a simple program, one that will get you up to speed quickly on the basics of setting up fields, managing records, and making reports. You can always move your data to a more powerful program later, but it makes no sense to spend weeks learning a high-powered program just so you can store a straightforward list of addresses.

There are basically two types of database programs. The simplest ones are called *flat-file databases* and let you work with information in just one file at a time. A flat-file database is all you'll need for storing addresses, recipes, information about your compact disk library, or other small collections of data.

The most powerful databases are called *relational databases.* With these, you can separate collections of data into different files (customer addresses in one file and customer orders in another, for example), have several files open at once, and move information among them. These programs are designed to handle complex jobs like order entry and accounting systems.

For example, say you're entering a new sales order. You enter a part number in the Sales Orders file. The database matches the part number with a part record in an Inventory file, grabs the part description from the Inventory file, enters it in the sales order record (so you don't have to type it), and reduces the quantity for that part in the Inventory file (so your inventory count is kept up to date). In a relational database, you can set all this up to happen automatically.

Relational databases are much more difficult to learn than flat-file databases, because you need to understand complex relationships between fields in different files. If you like the idea of storing standard information in one file and reusing it elsewhere but you don't want to dive into a relational database program, there's another alternative: flat-file programs that can do lookups. These let you create *lookup fields* that can grab information from another file. You could have your Orders file automatically take a customer's name and address from a Customers file and add it to the new sales order whenever you enter a customer number. The difference between a lookup field and true relational capability is that lookups are one-way; a lookup field can only take information. A relational database, in contrast, can take information from or send information to another file.

Confused? That's why you should start with a flat-file program. Learn the ropes. By managing information in one file, you'll begin to see how it might be useful to perform lookups or use a relational program.

Work Backward

There's more to creating a database file than just typing data into some fields. The fields, field attributes, and calculations you set up depend not just on the data you enter but on what you want that data to tell you. The best way to build a database file is to work backward. Decide what you want to know about your data (which customers are slow to pay, for example, or which addresses are in Connecticut), then figure out how the program will have to organize and manage your data in order for you to know those things.

Before you open a new file and start defining fields, sit down with some paper and think things through. Think about the categories you'll need and how you'll want to view, sort, select, and print your data. Write down what kinds of layouts and report formats you want to produce — customer order forms, mailing labels, form letters, invoices, bills of lading, whatever. Give each layout and report format a name. Under each name, make notes about how the format will look — which fields it will include, how they should be arranged, how records will be sorted, and what calculations you'll want to make. Next to the name of each field in a report format, put down the data type and any useful attributes it might have (standard values, etc.).

As you work on paper, you'll see your file taking shape. Each report format or layout you list will call for its own group of fields, its own arrangement of fields, its own sorts or calculations. Lots of report formats or layouts will have the same fields in them, so the work will go faster and faster as you move along.

After you've written down everything you can think of, begin a new file and follow your plan. Create the fields and design the layouts and report formats. You'll still probably run into some things you didn't think of, but you'll be a lot closer to a finished, working design for your file than you would be if you just opened a new file and started bashing around.

Make It Easy for Others to Use Your File

If you're setting up a database file for other people to use, they probably won't know as much about the program as you do. Various features of a database program can make it easier for others to enter or work with information.

Use Standard Values

If a field will always contain one of a fixed set of options, set the program up to display a list of those options when that field is selected. That way, a user can simply choose one of the options to enter data; he or she doesn't have to remember all the possible options for that field or worry about typing them correctly. If a field will usually contain the same value (a state code, perhaps), set the program up to enter that value automatically in each new record.

Automate Things

If your program lets you create *macros*, or *scripts* — commands that automatically execute a series of other commands — use these whenever possible. The more you can reduce the number of steps people have to follow, the less likely they are to screw things up.

For example, say you want a sales order report that shows the day's orders and the total sales at the end of each day. Making this report means selecting just the current day's orders from among all the orders in your database file, choosing the report format that displays the fields in the right arrangement, and printing the report. Without scripts or macros, you have to teach others how to select the day's records by telling the program to display all records with the current date, choose the proper report format, so the records and fields are displayed in the arrangement you want, and print the report. You also have to pray they remember to do all those things in the right sequence every day.

It's a lot easier for you to create a script named *Sales Report* or a macro that stores these steps and executes them with just one keyboard command. Then all the users have to do is choose the script name from a menu or press the keys to play the macro. The program will display a query screen so they can enter the current date (to select the day's records). Once they enter the current date, the program selects the records and prints the report. Users don't have to know how to display the query screen, find the right report, or choose the Print command, because the script or macro does all this for them.

Spell Out Procedures

Another way to help users is to include some instructions right on the data entry form. Such forms always contain the fields in which you enter data, but you can also type plain text outside the fields on a data entry screen, like this:

```
                  ┌─────────────────────┐
                  │   Item Entry Form   │
                  └─────────────────────┘

Item          Standard Gizmo    ┌──────────────────────────────────┐
Quantity      88                │ Choose New Record from the Edit menu │
Unit Price    $1.02             │ to add a new, blank record, then type │
Cost          $89.76            │ item name, quantity, and unit price to │
                                │ enter a new item. Choose Save from the │
                                │ File menu to save any changes.        │
                                └──────────────────────────────────┘
```

This form contains a descriptive title at the top and a box of instructions at the right that tells users what to do.

Hide Unnecessary Commands and Options

One way to minimize screw-ups is to make it impossible for others to do anything you don't want them to do. If your program lets you restrict access to menus, data entry screens, reports, or commands, use these controls to confine other users to areas of the program in which you want them to work.

In a personnel file, for example, everyone might have access to a staffing layout that shows each employee's name and department. In the same layout, however, there might be a salary field that you can't view unless you enter a special password. When someone tries to display a form or print a report that contains the salary field, the program generates a dialog box requesting the password, which must be entered before it will display that form or print that report.

Label Everything

Database files tend to be living, changing things. You might start with a handful of fields, one data entry form, and one report format, but as time passes, you want to do more with your information. You end up changing the data entry form or adding new ones, adding new report formats, and adding or changing fields to work with data in new ways. This is as it should be.

But often when you're in the throes of solving a new database problem, you forget to use adequate labels. If you create a report format called *Sales1* for a specific purpose today, you might forget what it's for by next Thursday, and a name like *Sales1* won't help remind you. Or you may create several calculation or summary fields with similar names, like *TotalSales*, *SumSales*, and so on, and after a while it's hard to remember which field makes which calculation.

Database pros maintain logs that explain exactly what each field, data entry screen, and report is for. You should do the same thing. List each field, data entry screen, and report by name and include a brief description of what it does and what it's for. You can keep your log in a word-processor file, in a notebook you place near the computer, or even in another database file.

Of course, if you're lazy like me, you probably won't keep a log, because it's too much work. So here's another suggestion: be as descriptive as possible with every field, data entry form, and report format name. Use names that tell what each thing is really for. Instead of *Sales Report* and *Monthly Sales Report,* try *1st Qtr. Sales by Region* and *March Sales by State.*

Finally, you can avoid confusion by keeping your database structure as tidy as possible. Check your collection of screen forms and report formats periodically and delete the ones you don't need anymore.

Conserve Paper Before You Print

Mastering database design can be a difficult and confusing process, but it's nothing compared to getting the right data to print on the right page. Every report seems to require two or three false starts before you get what you want.

Printing database reports is harder than printing other types of documents because there are so many more variables. As with word processing or spreadsheets, you have to make sure the right data is printing on each page. However, you also have to make sure you've selected the right set of records before you begin printing.

Here are a few tips that can improve your chances of getting a report right the first time. And remember, follow a routine. Most people are way too trigger-happy with the Print command. We finish doing one thing in the database and it's off to the printer. Then it comes out wrong. Slow down and follow these steps:

1. Make sure the information is correct. Display the records in a columnar layout on the screen, then sort the file on one field (the Last Name field in an address database, for example). Browse through the records on the screen and look for duplicate records, typos, and other data problems.

Sorting records helps you find duplicate records because it arranges them on top of one another in a list. For example, if you have duplicate records for Harry Schmidt and you sort the file on the Last Name field, you'll be able to spot the duplicates easily because they'll be next to each other. Fix any mistakes, eliminate any duplicates, and sort the records again in the order you really want, if necessary.

2. Select the records you want to print. Use the program's record selection or query functions to choose only the records you want. For example, if you only want to print records of customers from Pittsburgh, use the program's query function to select records in which the City field contains *Pittsburgh*. After you perform the selection or query, display the records in a list layout on the screen and scan the list, looking for any records that you don't want. If you find lots of unwanted records, your selection criteria might not be specific enough.

3. Check the report format. Once you're sure you have the records you want in the order you want, choose or create the report format you want. Check the format to see that every field you want is on it. Make sure the fields line up the way you want. Look closely: small alignment problems on the screen can look a lot bigger on paper.

You also use the report format options to determine the size of each report page and to set the page margins. This can be confusing when you're printing labels, because a sheet of address labels is probably 8½ by 11 inches (page size, so it fits in your printer), but each "page" in the database report is one label. There might be twenty or thirty report "pages" for each physical sheet of labels you print.

To avoid problems printing labels,

- **use a standard label.** Avery Label makes dozens of different label sizes, each of which has a stock number. Many database programs let you choose a label report format simply by choosing the Avery stock number that matches the stock you're printing on. This is by far the easiest way to get labels to print properly.
- **check margins.** Some sheets of labels have half-inch top and bottom margins, and other sheets don't. You have to account for these margins when you set up your report pages, or data will begin printing in the margin rather than in the first row of labels.
- **check label spacing.** Some label sheets have spaces between the labels, and others don't. If your labels do have spaces, the size of each label (one "page") is measured from the top of one label to the top of the label below it, so the space between the labels is included in the page size. In arranging fields on a label layout, make sure you arrange them so the data prints on the labels and not in the spaces or margins.
- **keep data away from the margins.** Move the fields on the report format so they're as close to the center of the label as possible. A field you lined up at the very edge of a label on the report format can end up off the label when the sheet of labels slips a bit in your printer. If necessary, make fields

smaller or use smaller type so there's some space between your data and the edges of the label.

4. Check the page setup and paper options. Choose the Page Setup command from your program's File menu and make sure you've specified the right paper size. Choose a paper size that matches the physical size of the sheets you're printing on.

5. Preview the report. If your program has a preview feature, look at the report on your screen. Watch for misaligned fields, fields that aren't wide or tall enough to display all their information, and missing fields.

6. Try a one-page test. If you can't preview a report, print one page of it to make sure the data fits on the page and is lined up properly. You can discover and fix most problems without printing a whole report.

If you're printing labels, print one page on regular paper and then hold it up to the light with a sheet of labels behind it. You should be able to see whether the addresses actually fall within the label boundaries. Printing test labels on paper is cheaper than wrecking sheet after sheet of label stock.

CHAPTER 10

Communications Credos

Communications Basics

Communications covers anything you do with your computer to exchange information with another computer. There are two basic types of computer communications: *network communications* and *remote communications.*

In network communications, your computer is connected to many other computers at the same time. A network links a group of computers and printers in an office, a company, a university, or a government agency. Networks vary in size from a few to thousands of computers.

In an office, for example, a *local area network* might connect your computer with other computers and printers by means of a cable. In a large corporation with offices around the country or the world, a *wide area network* uses cable, telephone connections, and even microwave and satellite links to connect the company's local area networks with one another.

A network connection is usually ongoing. Once you connect

to the network, the connection is maintained all day long, so you can communicate with other computers on it at any time. You can save files onto another computer's disk, get files from another computer's disk, or print your documents on a printer on the other side of the office.

In remote communications, your computer connects to just one other computer via a telephone line or a cable. Once the connection has been established, the two computers can exchange information. Remote communications are usually not ongoing. When you want to send or receive something, you establish a connection, transfer the information, and break the connection.

For both network and remote communications, you need special software and hardware. Communications software tells your computer how to send and receive information. Computers can exchange data in various ways, and communications software has settings that let you control exactly how it is being exchanged. For example, you can adjust the speed at which information is sent or received and the method by which your computer checks to make sure it has been transferred properly. When computers communicate, the software at both ends must use the same settings. Otherwise, it is like speaking English to someone who only understands Swahili.

Communications hardware includes the cables, boxes, and

> *Technically, it's possible to send computer data over digital tele-phone lines without a modem. These lines can carry computer data in the same form in which computers store it. There aren't very many digital lines around yet, but eventually all telephone lines will be digital and we won't need modems anymore.*

adapters you need to make a physical connection with other computers. On a local area network, your computer is con-nected to a network cable with an adapter that plugs into one of its *expansion slots* or *communications ports.* When you con-nect just two computers, you can either hook a cable directly between them (if they're close together) or make a *dial-up con-nection* over a telephone line.

To make a dial-up connection, you need a *modem,* a box or expansion card that plugs into one of your computer's internal slots or communications ports. A modem translates electronic data pulses from your computer into sounds that can be car-ried over ordinary telephone lines. To exchange information between your computer and a fax machine, you need a *fax modem,* which transfers data as a fax machine does. The mo-dem connects your computer and the phone line. Its speed is measured in bits per second, or *bps*. Different modems work at different speeds, but the most common ones are 2400 and 9600 bps.

Communications hardware and software work together: each is useless without the other.

How Networking Works

If you're hooked up to a local area network, you're in luck. This is the easiest kind of computer communications. Somebody called a network administrator is responsible for installing the networking software and hardware and for making the whole system work.

The network is easy to use. Each day you join, or *log on to,* it. Normally, you run a network software program to display a log-on dialog box, then type your name and a password to gain access to the network.

Once you've logged on to the network, you use the networking program's menus or dialog boxes to choose which other computers or printers you want to use. For example, if you choose, or *mount,* another computer's disk, that disk becomes available to your computer just as if it were inside your own computer.

In many cases, you'll also use a network to exchange *electronic mail* with other computer users. Each user has a unique network name and address where you can send mail.

There are two kinds of devices on a network. A *server* is a computer or printer that's available for others to share. The networking software you use to turn a computer or printer into a server is called *server software.* A computer can be set up as a *file server* (which makes its disks available for storage), a *mail server* (which stores and forwards electronic mail messages), or a *print server* (which manages printing jobs sent from network users to a particular printer).

A *client* is a personal computer that uses network servers. The software you use to connect with the network and use servers is called *client software.* Usually networks have a few servers and a lot of clients.

On Macintosh computers, you can make your computer a file server and a client at the same time. That means that you can simultaneously make your disk available on the network for others to use and connect to other users' shared disks.

Remote Communications with an On-Line Service

The easiest way to explore remote communications is to subscribe to an *on-line computer service.* These services, such as Prodigy, CompuServe, and America OnLine, are mainframe computers that offer all sorts of information and services once you're connected to them. You can use them for

- looking up information in encyclopedias, financial services reports, and other databases;
- playing games;
- exchanging electronic mail or files with other users of the service;
- retrieving, or *downloading,* programs;
- reading the latest news;
- looking up stock prices;
- shopping for merchandise;
- making airline reservations; and
- joining on-line discussion groups, or *forums,* to view and post messages on specific topics and share them with several other users at once.

Hundreds of individual users at a time can call into and use an on-line service. CompuServe and Prodigy are the largest, with more than two million subscribers each, but there are about a dozen major services out there, and many more smaller ones.

To connect to an on-line service, you need

- a modem, so you can dial the service's computer;
- the telephone number of the service's computer;
- a *terminal program,* which you use to make the call from your computer; and
- a *user name* and *password,* which identify you as a subscriber to the service.

When you subscribe to a service, you're given your own user name and password, along with the telephone number your computer must dial to reach the service's computer. Most major on-line services have local telephone numbers in every major city, so the call you make is usually a local one.

When you buy a modem, you usually get a general-purpose terminal program along with it. If you use this program, you must set it up to make the proper connection with the on-line service you're calling. However, the major services also give away or sell special terminal programs that are preset to connect with their computer. These special programs display specific menus, windows, and icons that make it easier to use the on-line service. In some cases — for America OnLine, for ex-

On-Line Charges and Access Charges

Subscribing to and using an on-line service can involve two different costs, the service charges you pay to use the service itself and the telephone charges for the phone call you make to connect with the service's computer.

You always pay the on-line service charges, no matter what. Usually you give the service a credit-card number when you subscribe, and the monthly charges show up on your bill. Different services have different fee structures, but the basic unit of service is an hour. Some services charge a flat monthly rate, others have a flat rate for a specific number of hours per month, and some simply charge by the hour.

Some on-line services give you access to a certain group of services for a flat monthly rate and charge extra for others. For example, you might be able to play a game or access sports news as part of what you get for the basic monthly rate, but looking up detailed financial information might carry a surcharge.

In addition to any service charges, you may also pay for the cost of the phone call that connects you with the service. If you're in a big city, the service probably has a local phone number you can dial. If you live in the country, however, the nearest access number might require a long-distance call. Any phone charges you incur in connecting with an on-line service are billed by your phone company.

ample — you can't call the service unless you use its special terminal program.

Once you've hooked up the modem to your computer and a phone line and you've installed the terminal program, you're ready to connect with the service. This involves the following steps.

1. Turn on your modem and start the terminal program on your computer.
2. Choose a command (usually called Setup or Connection Settings) to display a dialog box in which you enter the telephone number you want to dial, along with your user name and password.
3. Choose a command to make the call (usually Open Connection, Connect, or Dial). You'll probably hear a dial tone, dialing, and a roaring or screeching noise as the other computer answers the call.
4. You'll see a series of messages on your screen as you make contact. If you're using a general-purpose terminal program, you must type in your user name and password. If you're using a special terminal program designed for the service you're calling, the program automatically sends your user name and password to the other computer so it can verify your membership. Once your user name and pass-

word have been checked, you're granted access to the remote computer.

5. Click on icons or type or choose commands in your terminal program to use different features of the on-line service. The commands are sent to the service's computer, and it responds. For example, one command might display the hour's news headlines, while another might check your electronic mailbox for messages.

6. When you've finished using the service, hang up by choosing a command (usually called Sign Off, Disconnect, or Exit) to disconnect.

Remote Communications with Another Personal Computer

(Warning: This communications method is not for the technically faint-at-heart. If you want to send mail to or exchange files with someone else and both of you use an on-line service or a network, use that method instead. Both of them are much easier.)

If your computer and another computer you want to communicate with are close enough to each other, you can connect them directly with a cable plugged into each computer's serial port. To connect with another personal computer in a remote location, you use a dial-up connection and a modem.

Either way, you use a general-purpose terminal program that you can buy from a software dealer. Such a program isn't as easy to use as a special terminal program supplied by on-line computer services. Since it can be set to communicate with a variety of different computers, you must set it yourself to connect properly with the particular computer you're calling. This means you have to understand the program's settings and how to choose them. (See "Terminal Program Settings," p. 236, for more on these settings.)

Before you make a connection, talk to the other computer's operator and agree on the communications settings you'll be using. You don't have to use the same program as the remote computer has, as long as both programs use the same communications settings. You must also decide which computer will be making the call and which will be receiving it. Here's how the connection usually goes:

1. Turn on your modem and start the terminal program. If you don't automatically see a blank document window on your screen, open one by choosing the New command from the File menu.

2. With a document window open, use the program's menus

or commands to select the communications settings you've agreed upon and to enter the other computer's phone number (or to tell your program to answer the phone, if the other computer is calling you).

3. Choose a command (usually Open Connection, Dial, or Connect) to make the call. You'll hear a roaring or screeching from the modem as the other computer (or your computer) answers the call.

4. When the call goes through, you'll see a message like *CONNECT* on your screen to let you know you're hooked up. At this point, anything you type in your communications document window is sent to the other computer, and anything the other computer's operator types appears on your screen as you receive it.

5. First, type *Hello* or something to make sure the other person can read what you're sending. The other person types *Hello Yourself* or a similar response to let you know he or she can read what you're sending.

6. When you communicate in this mode, which is called *terminal mode,* all the data you exchange appears in the document window and is stored in a *buffer* (a part of your computer's memory). The document window fills up with the data you send or receive; the lines of data scroll off the top

Where Does the Internet Fit In?

The Internet isn't a computer and it isn't a network. It's a network of networks, a superhighway that links on-line services and computer networks at companies, universities, and government agencies all over the world. In all, more than ten thousand different networks and on-line services (and over 20 million users of those services and networks) are linked via the Internet.

Any user on an Internet-connected network can communicate with any other user on any other Internet-connected network. And not only can you exchange messages with other users, you can use the Internet to get an incredible amount of information from networks other than your own. For example:

- Many government agencies have networks on the Internet. You can access information about the census, business activity, congressional votes, the Library of Congress, and dozens of other topics.
- Most of the world's major universities have networks on the Internet. You can connect to file servers on those networks to search for specific research information.

of the window as new ones appear at the bottom. But because the text is stored in your computer's memory, you can scroll the document window up to see text you received earlier.

Instead of using the buffer to store all the information as

- Most of the world's major corporations and governments have networks on the Internet, so you can send messages directly to people such as Tom Brokaw at NBC News, Bill Gates at Microsoft, and Bill Clinton at the White House.
- On-line services are connected to the Internet, so if you subscribe to an on-line service, you can send electronic mail to anyone anywhere else on the Internet. Most on-line services are beginning to allow you to search for information over the Internet as well. You will usually pay more to send or receive mail or information this way than you would within the on-line service. Check your information service's manual for instructions.

If your computer isn't part of an Internet-connected network and you don't subscribe to an on-line service, you can still gain access to the Internet. *Internet services providers* charge a monthly fee to give individual users access to it. The provider's computer is connected to the Internet, and you dial into the provider's computer and get onto the Internet through it. These providers charge as little as $20 a month for this service.

it is sent or received, you can tell your terminal program to *capture* all the information, or save it in a file on your disk.

You can also use a terminal program to transfer whole files that you created previously with your word processor or other programs. To do this, choose a Send File command

and select the file you want to send, or choose a Receive File command and choose the location on your disk where you want the incoming file stored.

When you transfer a file, you don't see its contents in your document window as they go out. Instead, you see a message that tells you the file's name and size, how much of it has been transferred so far, and how much remains to be transferred.

During a file transfer, the terminal program uses a *file transfer protocol,* a set of transmission rules that helps make sure all the data is transferred properly. The terminal programs on each computer must be set to the same file transfer protocol.

After a file transfer is completed, the message on your screen says so and then disappears. You're returned to the document window, in which you can type more messages or issue other commands.

7. When you've finished communicating, you end the session by typing *So Long* or something like that, to let the other person know you'll be hanging up. Then you choose a command such as Close Connection or Hang Up to disconnect.

8. After you disconnect, you can scroll through your communications document to see information you received during the connection. Once you close the document, however, all

the information stored in the buffer is lost. Even if you save the document on your disk, only the particular settings you chose to make the connection are saved, not the information in the document window.

There are two ways to save information from your communications document window permanently. First, you can use your program's Capture Text command to save the information into a file on your disk as you receive it. Second, after you disconnect, you can select all the information in the window, choose the program's Copy command, open a new word-processing document, paste the information into that, and save that document to preserve the information.

Preventing Dial-Up Problems

The best way to prevent problems during dial-up connections is to set everything up properly to begin with.

Prepare outgoing files. If you're planning to send some files during your communications session, check them in advance to make sure they're in the proper format. The format you choose depends on how you plan to send the file and where you're sending it.

If you're sending a file to someone who wants to open it

with a different program, make sure the file is in ASCII, or text, format.

If you're sending a file through an on-line service that only accepts ASCII files, save the file in Text With Line Breaks format. (The service's manual will tell you if it only accepts ASCII files.) When you use the Text With Line Breaks format, each line you send has a return character at the end, so it will be exactly as long as it was in the document on your screen. Some information services have line length limits, so if you send an ASCII file without line breaks, each "line" is a whole paragraph long, and may be too long for the service to handle. (See p. 61 for more information on ASCII format.)

If your word processor uses graphic symbols (🍎) or other unique characters, open the ASCII version of the file and look at it on the screen before sending it. Sometimes, translating a file to ASCII format turns these characters into other characters — each 🍎 becomes a *p*, for example, turning 🍎 *Menu* into *p Menu.* Use your word processor's Find or Replace command to look for special characters like this and replace them with standard ones.

If you're sending a file in its native format rather than in ASCII format, you don't have to do anything special to it. Just make sure you're using a file transfer protocol that allows binary file transfers. (Unlike an ASCII file, a binary file can contain program instructions and graphics as well as letters and numbers. See p. 238 for more about file transfer methods and protocols.)

Check terminal program settings. Make sure you're using the same settings as the other computer. If you're in doubt, choose 8 data bits, 1 stop bit, and 0 parity bits for the data format and XModem for the file transfer protocol (see p. 239). These are the most common settings, and every terminal program has them. Make sure the modem settings match your modem setup. For example, don't set your program for 9600 bps speed if your modem only transmits at 2400 bps, and don't indicate that the modem is connected to the COM1 port when it's really connected to the COM2 port.

Check the physical connection. If you have an external modem, make sure the power cord is plugged in and the data cable is plugged into the right communications port on your computer. If your modem has two telephone jacks, make sure the cord that you plug into your wall jack is plugged into the correct jack on the modem.

Troubleshooting Dial-Up Connections

Here are some of the most common problems with dial-up connections and what to do about them.

Your modem doesn't dial, even though it's turned on. If nothing happens when you choose the Dial command in your terminal program, make sure your modem is on, type *ATA* in the document window, then press Return. If you have an external modem, you should see the status lights on its front blink momentarily. If you have either an internal or an external modem, your screen should show *OK* after you press Return.

If you do see a confirmation message or the modem's status lights flash when you type *ATA*, choose the Modem Settings command in your terminal program and make sure you've entered a phone number for the modem to dial.

If the status lights don't blink or you don't see a confirmation message on the screen, check the cable connections to make sure your modem is plugged in properly. If it is, choose the Modem Settings command in your communications program and make sure you've chosen the communications port setting that matches the port where your modem is actually connected. (For example, you might have chosen COM2 as the port when your modem is actually connected to COM1.) Look at the back of your computer to make sure that the port indicated in your terminal program is the one where your modem's data cable is actually connected. If you're using an internal modem, check its manual to make sure you've selected the correct port option in your terminal program.

If you still haven't found the problem, there may be something wrong with your modem.

It takes forever for your modem to dial a number, and you hear clicking as each number is dialed. Choose the Modem Settings command in your program and make sure the dialing method is set to Tone, not Pulse.

Your phone rings but your modem doesn't answer. Choose the Modem Settings command in your terminal program and choose the Auto Answer option.

Your call doesn't go through. Make sure that you hear a dial tone when the call begins and that the modem is actually dialing the number. You usually see the number on your screen as it's being dialed. If your modem has a speaker, you can hear the dial tone and the numbers being dialed, followed by rings and the other modem answering.

If you don't hear a dial tone, plug a regular phone into your phone jack and see if you hear it then; if you don't, you may have a dead phone jack.

If you hear a dial tone and the number is dialed but there's no answer, the other computer's modem may not be set to answer. You'll hear the phone ringing without being answered, or you'll see a message that your modem is dialing, but you won't see the *CONNECT* message that says the other computer answered the call. Check with the other computer's operator.

The call goes through, but you're disconnected right away. Your data format settings probably aren't the same as those on the other computer (see p. 236). Check with the other computer's operator, or check the on-line service's manual for the right settings.

You can't see what you type, or everything you type is doubled. Choose the Terminal Settings command in your program and change the Local Echo or Duplex setting from On to Off, or vice versa.

All the text you receive stays on one line that keeps rewriting over and over. Choose the Terminal Settings command in your program, and change the Autowrap or Auto Linefeed On Cr setting to On.

You see a lot of weird characters on the screen. Make sure your data format settings are the same as those on the other computer. If they are, the problem may be a noisy phone line. Hang up and try the call again. If the screen still shows weird characters, try making a regular phone call on the same line and listen for lots of static. Usually static affects one particular call, and it goes away if you dial again, unless there's an electrical storm in your area.

Incoming data has crazy margins, gaps, or a few weird characters in it. The other person hasn't formatted the data properly before sending it. Capture the incoming data to a file (using your program's Capture Text command) and then open it with your word-processing program, or copy the data from your communications document window to a word-processing document. Once the data is in a word-processing document, you can reformat it.

Incoming lines of text are all too short or too long. Choose the Terminal Settings command in your program and change the Line Length setting.

It takes forever to send or receive information, or for the other computer to respond to your commands. The other computer is probably busy. This is a common problem with on-line services, especially at night and on weekends, when they're handling lots of users at the same time. Be patient. Typing a command repeatedly won't make things go faster; it will just force the other computer to respond to the same command over and over.

When you scroll back up in your communications document, you can't find some information you received earlier. Your buffer is too small, so the information you received earlier has been forced out by information you received later. The earlier information is gone for good, but you can choose the Terminal Settings command and select a larger buffer size to avoid this in the future.

Your communications program says it's running low on

memory. Your buffer is too large. Choose the Terminal Settings command in your program and select a smaller buffer size or no buffer. Then choose the Capture Text command so all the data from your document window is automatically saved to your disk.

Network Niceties

A network is a community of users, and you should observe several basic matters of etiquette to avoid being branded antisocial.

Identify yourself. Don't use a silly or vague name to identify your computer, yourself, or a printer on the network. At first blush, you might want to use your first name only as an electronic mail address, or call your computer "Keisha's Computer." Depending on the size of the network, however, there may be more than one Keisha, and people might not be sure which computer belongs to which Keisha. If you're setting up a network printer, naming it Rover or Spike might be cute, but it doesn't tell anyone where it is or who it belongs to.

Don't be selfish. Don't stay connected to a particular server when you aren't using it. Every server has to work to manage each client's connection, so clients should try not to make life harder on the server than it needs to be. Whenever possible, copy files to your own disk before you open them to work on them. If you open a file while it is still on the server's disk, the server has to work to maintain the connection between your computer and its disk as you make changes to the file.

Respect other people's property. Network servers often contain files stored by lots of people. Don't be nosy. Don't look into other people's directories or files. Also, don't change file or directory names that somebody else set up. This is like going into a neighborhood at night and rearranging the street signs.

Don't copy software illegally. Network servers or disks shared on a network by individuals often contain lots of programs. Don't copy any of these to your own disk unless your company has a license that allows you to do so. Software piracy is a crime.

How to Keep On-Line Charges in Line

Using an on-line service can be really expensive. Sometimes, poking around on a service for hours and hours can result in a bill for $100 or more. Whenever you use an on-line service, remember that the meter is running. Here are some ways to keep connection costs down.

Know what costs extra. Before you connect and start exploring, check with your service to find out just which areas are covered under the standard rate and which carry a surcharge. Learn how to tell when you're moving from a standard-rate area to an extra-cost area (a notification usually appears on your screen when you do). Find out how many hours of service are covered under the flat monthly fee and whether you have to call at a certain time of day to be covered under the flat fee.

Know what you're going to do before you connect. The easiest way to run up a big bill is to wander aimlessly around an on-line service's computer without paying attention to the time or to which particular service you're using. You'll want to do a little exploring during your first few sessions just to get the lay of the electronic land, but try to limit these expeditions to an hour or less. After that, decide in advance which services you want to use, then head directly to them once you're connected.

Read and write off-line. When you find the information you're looking for, download it to your own computer and disconnect from the service before reading it. (There's usually a Get or Download command to do this.) When you read articles or electronic mail while you're connected, the time can go by quickly, and the connection charges can add up. Even if your time on the service is covered under a flat monthly fee, you may still be paying long-distance charges for the call you made to connect.

The same goes for sending electronic mail and transferring files to other people via the service. Write any messages and prepare any files before you connect, so you can simply send them once you're hooked up. This way, you can take your time writing and make sure everything is spelled properly without worrying about how much the connection is costing you.

Call during off hours. Most on-line services vary their charges by the time of day. Find out if your service is cheaper at night or on weekends and try to use the service when the rates are lowest.

Use an 800 number. The "local" access numbers provided by many on-line services aren't local calls in many parts of the country. If the nearest access number for your on-line service requires a long-distance call, find out if the service has an 800 number you can use instead. Some companies have a special 800 number but don't widely publicize it. You usually pay an hourly charge for calling in on this number. Ask your customer support representative if your on-line service has such a number.

Dial out of state. If your service doesn't offer an 800 number and your local access number is long distance, try calling an out-of-state access number rather than an in-state one. You usually pay more for in-state long distance (Columbus to

Toledo, for example) than for state-to-state long distance (Columbus to Indianapolis, for example).

Terminal Program Settings

This is the deepest, darkest, most technical part of this book. You can safely ignore this stuff if you're using a computer network or calling an on-line computer service with a special terminal program, but you'll need to know it if you're using a general-purpose terminal program to make a dial-up or direct connection.

Every terminal program has a range of settings you must choose to connect properly with another computer. There are lots of settings, but fortunately there are a few standard ones, and once you set them you can usually forget them.

Data Format Settings

Different computers like to receive data in different-sized chunks. Data format settings control the size of the data chunks that your terminal program sends to another computer. These settings have to be the same on your computer as they are on the other computer. The settings are

- *data bits* — the number of bits used for each chunk of data;

- *stop bits* — the number of bits used to separate chunks of data; and
- *parity bits* — bits that verify that each chunk was transferred properly.

The most common data format settings are 8 data bits, 1 stop bit, and 0 parity bits.

Modem Settings

These tell the terminal program how to work with the particular modem you're using.

Modem type tells your software which specific brand and model of modem you're using. The terminal program sends commands to make the modem take the phone off the hook, dial, answer, and transmit data. These commands can differ from modem to modem. For example, the command to dial a number might be ATDT on one brand of modem and ADT on another. A terminal program can send different commands for different brands of modems, but you have to tell it which modem you're using. Most modems utilize a standard set of commands called the *Hayes command set.* If your modem is listed among the options in your terminal program, choose it. Otherwise, choose the Hayes-compatible option; that should work.

Modem port tells the software which communications port

your modem is connected to on your computer (COM1 or COM2 on a PC, or the Macintosh modem or printer port, for example). If you're using an internal modem, check your manual to see which port setting you should choose.

Speed is the rate at which data is sent. Set this at or below your modem's top speed. For example, if the top speed is 2400 bps, don't set the terminal program to send data at 9600 bps.

Auto dial or *auto answer* determines whether the modem will dial or answer a call. You choose one or the other. If you set the modem to auto dial, you must also enter a telephone number for it to dial.

Redial or *answer options* set the number of times the modem will redial if it gets a busy signal, or the number of rings it will wait before answering an incoming call.

Tone or *pulse* dialing tells the modem to dial each digit in the number as a tone (like the ones you hear when you push the buttons on a touchtone phone) or as pulses (which mimics the way a rotary-dial phone dials). You usually choose the Tone setting.

File Transfer Protocols

The data format options discussed above control how information is sent from your screen to the other computer's screen. When you send complete files, however, you use other settings, or *file transfer protocols,* to exchange data. The most common file transfer protocols are XModem, Kermit, and ZModem.

Each protocol can transmit either ASCII files (which contain words and numbers) or binary files (which can contain program instructions or graphics as well as words and numbers). Once you've chosen a protocol, you must choose a *file transfer method.* For example, to send a native WordPerfect file to another computer, you might choose the Kermit protocol and the binary transfer method.

You don't necessarily have to understand how these protocols differ (you can find out in your terminal program's manual, if you're curious), but you must

- choose the same file transfer protocol that the other computer is using before sending any files (XModem, Kermit, or ZModem);
- choose the same file transfer method the other computer is using (ASCII or binary); and
- use the binary file transfer method when you're sending or receiving files in any program's native format.

Terminal Settings

These control how incoming and outgoing data looks in your document window. They don't affect the other computer, and they don't have to match the settings on the other computer.

Local echo or *Duplex* tells the program to display on your screen everything that is being sent. This setting is usually on. If you see double characters on your screen, though, turn it off.

Line length determines how long lines of text can be on your screen before they wrap around. This is usually eighty characters.

Autowrap (or Auto Cr on line feed) tells the program to begin a new line automatically when the current one is full.

The *buffer,* or scrollback area, size tells the terminal program how much memory to set aside for storing text as it scrolls off the top of your screen.

CHAPTER 11

Yikes! What Now?

Every Problem Has an Explanation

Most computer problems seem to come from out of the blue. There you are, trying to play by the rules, and suddenly the computer changes the rules (or, worse yet, it picks up the ball and goes home). But computers are like magicians: there's a perfectly good and reasonable explanation for everything they do, but what they do can seem miraculous because we don't understand what's really going on.

Rule number one in handling computer problems is this: **Every problem has an explanation, but often the explanation eludes us.** But take heart, because rule number one is inevitably followed by rule number two: **You can solve problems without explaining them.**

Of course, when some problem is preventing you from getting that report on the boss's desk or finishing your homework, these little mottoes may be little comfort. Here are two more points to keep in mind:

- Most computer problems are manmade. Human error is far and away the biggest cause of problems. Software and hardware are pretty reliable most of the time, and most of the problems you'll have are the result of some mistake you've made or some misconception you have about how the software or hardware is working.
- You can and will recover from any computer problem. There's little you can do with a computer that can't be put right. You can reset formatting, recalculate mistakes, and undelete files. Even if you trash your hard disk, there are companies that specialize in recovering data from it. There's no way you can electrocute yourself or annihilate the planet by messing up a formula in Excel. So whatever happens, it's not the end of the world.

With this perspective in mind, here's what to do when trouble strikes.

Don't Panic

When you have a computer problem, the worst thing you can do is panic. Panic makes it impossible to approach the problem rationally. So get over the initial shock, take a deep breath, and start tackling the problem with your mind rather than your emotions.

Classify the Problem

Start zeroing in on a solution by putting your problem into one of three broad classes: human error, software problems, and hardware problems. Once you've classified the problem, you can try an appropriate set of solutions.

Human Error

This is the most likely problem. You chose a command expecting one result and you got a different result. You see a screen you're not familiar with and you're not sure how to get out of it.

The basic test for human error is whether or not the computer and program are still working. If they are, the problem is probably human error. To find out, try moving the mouse pointer on the screen, clicking the Cancel button in a dialog box, or moving the cursor by pressing arrow keys. If the program responds to these actions, then it's still running and your task is to figure out what you did wrong. See "Conquering Human Error," p. 245.

Software Problems

A software problem causes the program to stop working. There are several symptoms of this.

In a *crash*, you see an error message on the screen or the screen fills with random characters or lines. Sometimes you can quit the program and return to the operating system screen, but usually your only option is to restart the computer.

In a *spontaneous quit*, the program closes itself and you're returned to the operating system screen.

In a *freeze*, the program doesn't look any different on the screen, but it locks up so you can't move the mouse pointer or cursor.

See "Fixing Software Problems," p. 247, for solutions to these problems.

Hardware Problems

A hardware problem usually reveals itself pretty clearly with strange sights, sounds, or smells. Some symptoms are

- a dim, discolored, shrunken, or distorted image on your monitor;
- whining, crackling, buzzing, or grinding noises from your monitor, system unit, disk drives, or printer;

- the smell of melting plastic from inside your monitor, system unit, or printer; or
- intermittent problems opening or saving files, viewing the contents of disks, or printing.

If you have one of these symptoms, you'll probably need to have the component checked out and repaired by a professional. However, you can check some things yourself before resorting to outside help. See "Fixing Hardware Problems," p. 252.

Conquering Human Error

Human error problems are the most difficult to overcome, because we're really talking about overcoming confusion based on ignorance. In most cases, the only remedy is to learn. The suggestions in Chapter 5 will help you build your understanding and avoid making mistakes. However, if you find yourself in a situation you don't understand and you've determined that the software and hardware are still working, here are some specific remedies to try.

Press Esc. If you suddenly see an unfamiliar dialog box or screen, try pressing the Esc key. This will often close the dialog box or return you to the main program or document screen.

Even if pressing the (Esc) key doesn't work, it won't hurt anything to try it.

Click the Cancel button. If you suddenly see an unfamiliar dialog box, click the Cancel button to put it away.

Undo it. The Undo command is at the top of the Edit menu in most programs, and it usually cancels the last action you took. So if you choose a command or perform an operation and you don't like the result, choose Undo to go back to where you were before.

Check the instructions. The instruction manual is often the last place we look for answers. Instead, we try different solutions on our own or ask people who know even less about computers than we do. But this type of guesswork can easily make things worse.

When you're confused, ask yourself, *What was I trying to do? Did I do it, or did I do something else by mistake?*

Before you pick up the manual, look at the screen carefully. Sometimes instructions about your options on a given screen are displayed at the bottom of the screen itself. Even if they're not, look at the top of the screen or dialog box for a title, so you'll know how to identify the part of the program you're in. You'll have a hard time deciding what to check in the manual if you don't know which part of the program you're in.

Retrace your steps. If you know you haven't chosen an im-

Take a Break

If you're getting frustrated or angry when a problem doesn't yield to a quick solution, step away from the problem for a while and calm down. Just get up and walk away from the computer for a couple of minutes. Think about something else. Once you clear away frustration and anger, you can return to the problem and calmly proceed with the next step in the solution process.

proper command to cause the current problem, think back to what you were doing or what settings you changed before the problem occurred. We tend to think about each thing we do on a computer as a separate task, but really they're like links in a chain of events. From the time you turn the computer on, many of the things you do can have subsequent effects. For example, you might adjust the memory for one program only to find later that this plays havoc with another program.

Fixing Software Problems

With a software problem, the computer is getting the wrong instructions from a program, not from you. Here are some remedies to try.

Try the command again. If you get an error message or a command doesn't seem to work, it's always worth trying the procedure again. Some minor problems are temporary and will have resolved themselves by the time you choose the command again.

Know your setup. Some software problems occur because your system software isn't adjusted properly; a new setting you choose causes a conflict with settings that existed before. You can't possibly know what's wrong unless you know what's right. Take the time to understand the standard system software settings for your computer.

If you're using a PC, open your DOS manual or a good DOS book and read about the commands in the AUTOEXEC.BAT and CONFIG.SYS files. Use a word-processing program to open these files on your hard disk, and print each file out so you'll know what commands it contains for future reference.

If you're using Windows, pick up a good book about Windows and read about the Program Manager, File Manager, and Print Manager to learn about their settings and how to change them.

If you're using a Macintosh, get a book about the system software and learn about the standard System Folder contents and Finder and Control Panel settings and how to change them. Notice which modifier programs (*control panels, extensions,* or *inits*) come with the standard system software, so you can tell which of the ones in your System Folder didn't come from Apple. (Usually third-party system software additions cause the most problems.)

Check and change your setup. Once you're familiar with operating system settings, check them when there's a problem. A setting you changed earlier may be causing the problem now.

Restart the program. Minor problems with an application program can be fixed by saving the document(s) you have open, quitting the program, and restarting it. If the program has managed to scramble itself temporarily while running, this will straighten it out.

Restart the computer. If restarting a particular program doesn't help, restart the whole computer. Restarting the computer is shutting it off and turning it on again. It empties the RAM of instructions, flushing out any bad instructions that may have caused a problem, and returns your computer to its pristine state. This will take care of minor problems with the operating system software. If you can, save any open files before you restart, but if a program is frozen or has crashed, this probably won't be possible.

Open a backup copy of the file. If a file is doing funny things — commands aren't working, or the screen display is messed up — and restarting the program doesn't help, try opening a backup copy of the file. It could be that the file is garbled. If you don't have a backup copy, save the current file under a different name, close it, then open the newly named file.

Use a virus checker. Your problem could be caused by a computer virus. The easy way to eliminate this possibility is to run a virus-checking program to scan your hard disk and floppy disks for infections. If you find infections, you should be able to repair them with the same program.

Reinstall the program. If restarting the program doesn't solve your problem and the problem doesn't seem to happen with other programs you use, reinstall the program from its original floppy disks. Over time, a program's files on your disk can become slightly garbled, so that your CPU can't read the instructions properly. Reinstalling the program will clear this up.

Return to vanilla. If restarting or reinstalling the program doesn't work, you may have a conflict between different pieces of software or with the system software settings that are in effect. Because there are a lot of settings, it can be difficult to figure out which of them is causing the problem.

If you don't know which setting is responsible, return all your computer's operating system settings to their factory, or *default,* settings and then see if the problem goes away. (Check your operating system manual to learn the default settings.)

If you're using a PC, you can either restore your original

> *Fixing the problem is what counts, not explaining it. If you can clear up a problem quickly and the problem doesn't return, don't worry about what caused it.*

AUTOEXEC.BAT and CONFIG.SYS files from your master system software disks or copies you made, or restart the computer with a system floppy disk.

If you're using a Mac, check your user's guide to see what the normal settings are for each of the control panels. If this doesn't work, eliminate any nonstandard control panel, extension, or init programs you may be running by dragging them outside your System Folder and restarting.

If the problem goes away after you return to vanilla, you'll know that some combination of commands or settings in your system software has caused the problem. Then start making changes, one at a time, to return the system to the way you had it set up before the problem occurred. When the problem reappears, you'll know that the last setting or command you made is the culprit.

Replace the system software. If restoring your system software settings to their factory defaults doesn't fix things, there's probably a problem with one of your system software files —

one of them has become garbled, so its instructions aren't correct anymore. Reinstalling the system software will fix this. The best way to do this is to start up your system with a different disk (or the original system software installation disk), erase the existing DOS or Windows directory or System Folder from your hard disk, and install a completely new set of system software files. (Be sure to erase the old system software files first, because installing a new set without erasing the existing ones won't always clear up the problem, and it can even make things worse.)

Fixing Hardware Problems

Here are two things to try before taking your computer to the repair shop.

Use a disk diagnostic program. If you're having trouble finding a file, opening a file, or saving a file, or the file you open doesn't contain the information you expect, run a disk diagnostic program, such as Norton Utilities, PC Tools, or Disk First Aid. These programs will tell you if there's something wrong with your disk or with a particular file, and they can usually repair minor problems as well.

Shut off the computer and check all the cables. If you're having intermittent problems getting or saving files on external disk drives, using an external modem, or printing, you may have a cable problem. Shut off the computer and all its external components and check every cable. Remove the cables one at a time and look inside each plug for bent pins. Straighten any that you find, if possible, or replace the cable. Make sure each cable is plugged in snugly and hasn't worked loose. If the problem is still there after you restart the computer, shut it off again and try replacing each cable with one that you know is okay.

Seeking Expert Help

If you can't resolve a problem on your own, you'll want to get some expert help. Most people who use computers know very little about how they work, so when it comes to finding advice or a repair shop, it can be hard to tell the experts from the impostors.

Here are the alternatives.

Friends and coworkers. It's easiest to ask somebody you know, especially if he's sitting at the next desk. Your coworker might have lots of experience with the same program you're having problems with. On the other hand, a coworker who doesn't know much might steer you wrong.

In-house experts. If your company has a computer support staff, you'll usually call them if you can't get an answer from somebody nearby. But even paid support people might not have a clue. If your company primarily uses Windows-based systems, for example, the company expert may know less than you do about your Macintosh. However, the support person should at least help you get in touch with someone who really can help you.

The manufacturer's technical support staff. Every hardware and software product you buy has some form of technical support available by phone. In most cases, the support itself is free, although the phone call may be long distance. In other cases, you get free support for only ninety days; after that you have to pay a fee for help. Any major problems you're having with software can usually be resolved within the first ninety days. With hardware problems, the support is usually free indefinitely.

Some companies offer great technical support, and others have terrible support. Your experience can even vary from call to call with the same company. Still, these support staff people can quickly resolve the most common problems. Before you call for technical support, however, prepare yourself so the call goes as smoothly as possible. See "On Seeking Technical Support," p. 256.

Authorized dealerships. If your computer or other hardware component is sold through a nearby authorized dealer, you can take it there for help. Dealers usually don't know much about software; you're better off calling the manufacturer's help line, unless the problem is with networking software, an accounting system, or some other complex package that the dealer installed for you and agreed to support.

Even with a hardware problem, authorized dealers are only a good bet if your broken component is under warranty and the repair will be free. If it isn't, you'll pay more to have it fixed at a dealership than at an independent repair shop.

Technicians at dealerships are trained to spot the most common problems and fix them with the least hassle. This usually means running a company-supplied diagnostic program and following a few steps to replace a whole logic board, or *subsystem,* instead of tracking down the chip or circuit that's really causing the problem. The result is that you pay for a whole board when you really only need one chip, or maybe just a solder joint repair.

Independent repair shops. There are now a lot of independent repair shops that specialize in fixing computer hardware. Most of them also sell used computers, because they can buy a broken system, fix it cheaply, and sell it at a profit.

Ask around for recommendations about repair shops near you. If there aren't any, pack up your system and send it off to one that you know can fix it. It's better to pay a freight bill and wait a few days for a repair than to waste your time and money at a TV repair shop down the street that is willing to take a stab at computer repair.

User groups. A good, large, long-established user group generally knows more about solving problems than any other organization. End users of a product, as a group, have vastly more experience with problems than any technical support staffer, dealer, or repair facility. It stands to reason that the people who use a product the most, and in the widest variety of ways, will know most about what goes wrong with it. User groups aren't afraid to tell you that a program has a bug. User groups aren't afraid to tell you that one repair shop stinks and another is great. User groups are the only organizations that have no vested interest in putting you off or overcharging you.

On Seeking Technical Support

Computer magazines and on-line computer services abound with horror stories about the quality of technical support available for computers and software. But while the experience can be decidedly unpleasant, there are ways to improve your chances of getting the help you need as efficiently as possible.

Know your system. Before you ask anyone for help or pick up the phone to call a technical support line, write down the details of your hardware and software setup. The setup can make a difference to how the technician diagnoses the problem, so write down the model of computer or other component (or the processor model, if it's a PC), the amount of RAM and hard disk space, the system software version you're running, and the version of the program you're having trouble with, if it's a software problem.

Know what you did. If possible, write down the steps you took — settings you changed, files you opened, or commands you chose — before the problem occurred. These can be a big help to the technician trying to diagnose your problem.

Have your computer running when you make the call. Most remedies for software problems involve doing things with the computer. Support technicians usually assume you're sitting at the computer and are ready to try whatever suggestions they offer. Don't waste your time or the technician's time by calling when you're nowhere near the computer or when it's not running.

Be patient. You will probably spend at least some time on hold, waiting for a support technician, so expect a delay. In some cases you'll be on hold for fifteen minutes or more. If you hate being on hold and the problem isn't critical, leave a message or fax a note about your problem to the company. In most cases, you'll get a response within a day or two. Also, if you subscribe to an on-line service, you may find an answer to your

Do You Need an Extended Warranty?

Every new computer comes with a warranty, but retailers will often try to sell you an extended service contract that offers on-site service or a longer warranty period, or both. Whether it's worth the money depends on your situation. Before we consider different scenarios, though, let's look at the facts about computer reliability and warranty coverage.

First of all, computer hardware is pretty reliable. If your computer has been run for at least twenty-four hours, or *burned in*, before you get it (and nearly all computers are), the factory or the dealership will have noticed most of the problems and repaired them already.

Second, the parts that are likely to break on a computer aren't that expensive to fix. The mechanical parts — floppy and hard disk drives — are the most likely to fail, and you can buy a pretty big hard disk for a few hundred dollars. Therefore, paying $200 or so for an extended warranty to cover a couple of $200 components may not make sense.

problem on a technical support forum the company has set up there. Otherwise, you can leave a message on the forum asking for help via electronic mail.

Be polite. This may seem like common sense, but it's easy to abandon courtesy when you're in the throes of a problem. Even if you're going nuts over something or you're steamed about

Equipment warranties cover either on-site or off-site repairs. On-site coverage is best, because the vendor promises to send someone to your computer to fix it. You don't have to get the computer back to the company. But this kind of coverage usually costs more, and may not be worth it if you're not likely to be in a huge hurry to get your computer up and running again.

If you're a casual computer user, take your chances with the manufacturer's warranty. If you can tolerate having your computer out of action or off the premises for a few days, then don't pay extra for on-site service.

If you use the computer to run a small business, you should probably get on-site service, even if you have to pay extra for it. Try to get a deal that supplies you with a replacement system if yours can't be fixed within twenty-four hours.

If you work for a big company, the company will probably have its own service setup. Large companies with lots of computers often negotiate their own deals with third-party service companies.

having to spend twenty minutes on hold, don't take it out on the technician. Getting all huffy about your problem will only make it harder to solve.

Be specific. Explain what the problem is. Be as specific as possible. It's not very helpful to say, "My screen is all messed up." Explain what command you chose or what else you were doing when the problem occurred. If you can, go back a little bit and tell the technician what you were doing before the problem came up.

Follow directions. Listen carefully to the technician's suggestions and do what he or she suggests, even if you think you've already tried it. You may be convinced you've already tried a certain remedy, but the technician has to be convinced of this before he will suggest another remedy. Also, he may suggest a slight variation that will make all the difference.

Press for a solution. Computer support people talk with dozens of callers every day. Most of the time, your problem is familiar and they have a solution ready. If your problem is an obscure one, however, the technician may eventually try to weasel out of helping you. She may suggest that the problem lies with another program or piece of hardware you're using, or that it's caused by a virus, or that nobody has ever had that problem before.

If at all possible, don't hang up without some marching orders. Ask for some specific remedies to try on your own. That way, if the problem still isn't resolved after you've tried all the suggestions, you'll be able to call back and say so, and perhaps get some more suggestions. And get the technician's name so you can talk to the same person again if you need to call back.

Be flexible. Nobody knows everything that can go wrong

with a computer system or a program. Nobody. Nevertheless, hardware and software gurus can frequently help you, because they've figured out how to help other people in similar circumstances. Your problem may sound a lot like somebody else's problem, and they might have a solution you can try. Or they may have a generic, if-all-else-fails solution that will work for your problem and countless others.

It doesn't matter whether the solution is what you expected or whether it explains the problem. All that matters is whether it works.

CHAPTER 12

Technology Marches On

You Can't Stop Technology

Gordon Moore, one of the cofounders of Intel Corporation, the world's largest manufacturer of computer microprocessors, once proposed the theory that microprocessors get twice as powerful or half as expensive every eighteen months. This theory is now called Moore's Law, and it has been pretty much true since the mid-1970s as the rocket of semiconductor technology has soared ever higher.

Moore's Law has two results. First, it makes computers accessible to more and more people, because the machines are becoming cheaper and easier to use. Second, it allows computers to do more and more things. Twenty years ago it was a big deal to be able to make a personal computer add up two numbers. Now you can make a multicolor chart from those numbers, and that chart can dance, talk, and check itself for spelling errors.

This trend toward faster, cheaper, and more capable computers will probably continue for the next several decades. But even though computer companies come out with new stuff all the time, the number of really important changes in computing over the past two decades can be counted on one hand. There haven't been any significant changes in the word processor I use for nearly ten years now. I know people who are still using computers they bought in 1985. These people have never discovered hard disk drives, multiple megabytes of memory, color screens, and other enhancements, but the computer still does the job for them. Even large companies that invested heavily in mid-1980s PC and Macintosh systems have found ways to continue using them productively.

Any computer system represents a certain level of capability. If the capability suits your needs, then it really doesn't matter whether the computer is five weeks old or five years old. If the capability doesn't meet your needs, though, even the latest model is the wrong one for you.

The New Computer Reality Check

Most people who bought a computer a year or two ago probably don't need a new one. Still, you may be getting the itch every time you walk by that new beauty at the electronics store. Let's look at what makes you want a new computer and whether or not that's a good reasons to get one.

It's faster! This month's model runs at 90 megahertz, so it blows the doors off last month's model, which runs at a poky 50 megahertz. If you're doing color photo rendering or video work, the increase will help you work faster. But if you're doing word processing, it won't make any difference at all.

It does more! New computers can display photo-quality color, play video clips, and recognize your voice, but if you spend most of your day using a word processor or spreadsheet, none of this will matter much. Features like this make computers more expensive, more difficult to set up and learn about, and more likely to break down. It's like buying a car that remembers three position settings for a power driver's seat when you know you'll be the only driver most of the time.

So think long and hard about whether you need that new computer. Don't be suckered by all this "latest, greatest" business.

If It Ain't Broke, Don't Fix It

You can thumb through a computer catalog or browse in a computer store and find all sorts of gizmos that will "fix" some of the "problems" your aging computer has developed.

- Disk utility programs make working with disks and files more convenient.
- Font programs help your computer display more kinds of type in a wider range of sizes.
- Memory management utilities let you run larger programs or more programs at once.
- Accelerators or replacement processors make your computer run more quickly.
- Alternative pointers, trackballs, digital tablets, and touch-sensitive pads give you better control with Windows or on a Mac.
- Alternative keyboards offer more keys and more convenience.
- Larger monitors show more information at a time.
- Larger, faster hard disks and removable storage devices offer more storage.

Whatever your problem is, there's a solution out there for it. The trouble is that these solutions can get expensive, they often complicate your system, and they probably won't have the miraculous effect you're looking for.

If you have a specific problem that seriously affects your ability to get things done on your computer, then by all means fix it. But don't look for problems. If the computer is doing its job, leave well enough alone.

Polish that Keyboard

It's a lot cheaper to make the most of what you have than it is to buy something new. When you first got your computer, it was the wonder of the ages. Here are two ways to recapture the romance.

Clean it up. Wipe that grunge off the keyboard and the cabinet. Clean the display screen. Take your mouse apart and clean the roller ball and socket — maybe you can get rid of that squeak or hesitation this way. If your computer's fan is noisy, maybe you can clean it or replace it.

Optimize it. Check the system software instructions for ways to make your system run faster or more conveniently. If you're tired of typing *CD* every time you want to switch directories on your PC, for example, add a PATH statement to your AUTOEXEC.BAT file so it's easier to start up programs you use a lot. If your computer has a hard disk *cache* — a special part of memory that stores frequently used instructions so they don't have to be read from the disk each time — see if you can make it larger by changing a system software setting; this might speed up your computer a little. If you have a diagnostic program, check your disk for file fragmentation. If you have serious fragmentation, you can speed up disk access by defragmenting it.

Three Reasons to Upgrade

If making better use of what you have still isn't enough, the next thing to consider is upgrading. By adding some memory, a larger hard disk, a different monitor, or even a new processor, you can make big changes in your computing experience.

Here are three key reasons to upgrade rather than buy a new computer.

1. You're basically happy with the computer you have. Admit it, you love the little gizmo. You've spent months or years setting it up just the way you like it. The disk files and desktop icons are just where you want them, and you know your way around the system like the back of your hand. You've invested a lot in the relationship, so the natural thing is to try to salvage it. If the only thing standing between you and total computing bliss is a little more RAM or a bigger hard disk, then by all means get the upgrade.

2. Upgrading is cheaper than buying a new computer. Unless you need to upgrade everything inside your computer (the processor, video system, memory, and disk), it's probably far cheaper to upgrade than to buy a new one. A newer version of your operating system will cost less than $100. You can buy some extra RAM or a bigger hard disk for only a couple of hundred dollars.

It's possible to pour more money into upgrades than your computer is worth, however. Here's a good way to decide. Find out the market value of your old computer and add to this the cost of any upgrades you're planning. If the total you come up with is 90 percent or more of the price of a new computer, it's probably wiser to get the new computer.

3. Upgrading is easier than buying a new computer. Most hardware upgrades are painless: you stick in some more RAM or an accelerator card, change a few DOS commands in your CONFIG.SYS or AUTOEXEC.BAT file (if you're using a PC), and bingo, you get more memory or speed. Upgrading the operating system software can be a bigger hassle, but even if it requires a lot of learning (moving from DOS to Windows, for example), you're no worse off than you'd be with a new system.

Upgrading also allows you to keep whatever disk organization and files you've spent months or years setting up. Even if you're switching to a larger hard disk, you can copy all your stuff from the old hard disk to the new one or use a backup program to record the contents and organization of your old disk and move them to the new disk. With a new system (which will probably have a different version of the operating system), you'll probably have to set up folders or directories all over again, decide which operating system files to keep and which to throw away, figure out which of your programs are compatible with the new computer, and upgrade the programs that won't work with it. It's a lot more trouble, and it's probably more expensive than you think.

What Are You Getting Into?

Before adding any new piece of hardware or software to your computer, think not only about what it will do but about how it will affect your current setup.

Everything you add to a computer has consequences. At the very least, you'll use up more disk space (and many of today's programs hog disk space like you wouldn't believe). But you might also have to make changes to your system software that will cause problems with other programs.

For example, you might install a pop-up appointment calendar program that appears at the touch of two keys, but this program may use just enough memory so that your word processor no longer has room to run its spelling checker or thesaurus.

Here are some questions you should answer before you buy.

Does the program run with your operating system software? Many programs require a certain version of DOS, Windows, or Macintosh system software to run. Upgrading system software is not a trivial matter, and the need to do so may cause you to think twice about that new program or gizmo.

Does the program need more RAM than you have? RAM has come down in price over the years, but you could still end up having to spend a couple of hundred dollars to add more memory to your computer in order to run certain new programs.

Will the program work with your monitor and video sys-

tem? Video systems are more expensive than RAM. If you need to upgrade your video display system just to run a new program, you might be better off shopping for a whole new computer instead.

Will your new hardware require other hardware changes? A new game may require a different joystick or controller from the one you have now, or it may sound awful unless you buy a sound card or a set of speakers to go with it. Or maybe you want to add a new component and all your computer's connection ports are in use already. In this case, you'll need to buy a switch box to accommodate the new component, or else unplug one device and plug in another each time you want to switch.

Find out the whole story before you buy. Some compatibility problems (printer drivers, conflicts with system software files, conflicts with other programs you run) aren't obvious and definitely won't be spelled out on the box of that new product. But there's another way to protect yourself. Tell the salesperson how your computer is set up and ask if it will work with what you're buying. If the salesperson says it will, get permission to return the product if it doesn't. That way, if you find that adding this one product will force you to change lots of other things, you can back out of the whole deal.

One Thing at a Time

Adding anything to a computer changes it in some way. Adding more than one thing at a time changes the computer in many ways, so if a problem occurs, it's hard to tell which change caused it. If you buy a game and a disk utility and a new sound card, install them one at a time. Restart the computer after you install each product, and try the product to make sure it's working properly. In addition, run some of your unrelated programs just to make sure they're still working too. Once you've made certain that the latest addition hasn't caused a problem, add the next product. Repeat the testing procedure with it.

This may seem like a lot of trouble, but it's the only way to isolate the sources of problems.

Three Reasons to Keep Your Old Computer

Even if you've decided to get a new computer, there are plenty of reasons to keep the old one around.

The old computer can serve as a backup. I've kept an old computer as a reserve system in case my current one breaks. I may not be able to display as many colors on the screen, but I can still use the old warhorse for word processing, spreadsheets, and other chores.

You won't get much for your old system if you sell it. Used computers aren't worth much, particularly if they're more than two or three years old.

You may be asked for support after the sale. If you sell or give the computer to a friend or acquaintance, that person will probably ask you for help. If he or she has never used a computer at all, you may find yourself doing a lot more hand-holding than you bargained for.

Two Reasons to Get Rid of Your Old Computer

Nonetheless, there are two good reasons to get rid of that old computer when you buy a new one.

A computer is a terrible thing to waste. If you know the computer will just be gathering dust in the closet or garage and you don't want or need a backup system, then by all means get rid of it so somebody else can use it. Remember that your old computer did a lot of good work for you. It can still do those things. Maybe someone else in your organization or house can use it, someone whose needs aren't as demanding as yours. My old computers have gone to my son, to my wife, to schools, and to friends. These computers were no longer powerful enough for me, but they've met the needs of many other people.

You need the money. Okay, so maybe $300 isn't such a bad deal. Maybe you can use it to get that CD-ROM player for your new system or to buy a better monitor or printer.

Four Ways to Get Rid of Your Old Computer

When you decide to get rid of your old computer, you have several alternatives, each with its own pros and cons.

Sell it to a friend. The good news is that you may be able to make an easy sale without having to advertise. The bad news is that you'll probably give your friend a better deal than you would a stranger, and you'll probably end up answering a lot of questions after the sale. The best situation is to sell it to a friend who already knows all about computers and is just looking for a second system.

Sell it to a stranger. You stick an ad in the paper or on a bulletin board somewhere and people call up, ask you questions for fifteen minutes, make appointments to come over, and don't show up. Others tromp through your house or office, play with your dog, check out your furniture, and spend half an hour looking your system over and trying to make up their minds. This is a lot to go through, especially if you're selling an old computer for $500 or less. But, you're not obliged to help strangers after the sale.

Sell the Computer, Not Your Data

You wouldn't sell a filing cabinet with your financial records still inside it, so don't leave your data on the computer's hard disk when you sell it. If you simply delete your files from your hard disk, you don't wipe the files off it. Deleting files in the normal way only removes information about their location from the disk directory; the computer can't find the files anymore, but they're still there. Someone else could use a disk utility program to locate them and "unerase" them.

Instead of deleting files or programs, reformat your hard disk before selling your computer. Reformatting really, truly removes all your files from the disk. It also gives you a chance to return the operating system's settings to their factory defaults, so the new owner can start with a clean, unmodified setup.

Sell it to a used computer store. Here you'll get a quick, hassle-free sale, but you'll only get about half as much as you would from a private party.

Give it away. You get the warm feeling of doing a good deed — plus a tax write-off, if you give the computer to a nonprofit group. Unless you're otherwise involved in the organization, you won't be asked for support. And if the organization does ask you for help and you choose to give it, you'll feel like a saint.

Glossary

This glossary will help you understand the meanings of technical words shown in italics throughout the book. When a definition here contains a word in italics, that word is also defined in the glossary.

Absolute cell reference. A *cell reference* in a spreadsheet *formula* that always refers to one specific *cell,* no matter where the formula appears.

Address. The location of a spreadsheet *cell,* designated by the letter-number combination of the row and column whose intersection the cell represents.

Address box. An area above a spreadsheet's row-and-column matrix that shows the *address* of the currently selected *cell.*

Answer option. A setting in a *terminal program* that determines if and how the program answers incoming telephone calls.

Application program (or **application**). A *program* that lets you perform a certain kind of job, such as writing, calculating, drawing, or playing a game.

ASCII (American Standard for Information Interchange) **format.**

A method of recording computer data that contains only letters, numbers, and punctuation symbols and that can be recognized by any *program*.

Attribute. A data-handling characteristic of a database *field*, such as its *data type*.

Auto answer. The ability of a *terminal program* to detect an incoming telephone call and answer it.

Auto dial. The ability of a *terminal program* to dial a telephone number.

AUTOEXEC.BAT file. A *file* that is loaded by the *operating system* when you turn on a *PC-compatible computer* and that commands the operating system to perform specific tasks, such as loading other *programs* automatically.

Autowrap. A *terminal program*'s ability to display data on a new line in a communications *document window* when the current line is full.

Binary file format. A *file format* that can store graphics and program instructions as well as text characters.

Bit. A binary digit, either 0 or 1.

bps (bits per second). The measurement of speed at which data is transferred by a *terminal program* or *modem*.

Buffer. A portion of the computer's *memory* set aside for storing data transferred in *terminal mode* with a *terminal program*.

Buffer size. An option in a *terminal program* that determines how much memory is set aside for the *buffer*.

Burning-in. Running a new computer system for twenty-four hours before it is sold or delivered, to make sure it is working properly.

Button. An item in a *graphical user interface* that can be *clicked* with a *mouse* to issue or confirm a command. See *Command, Clicking, Graphical user interface, Mouse.*

Byte. The basic unit of information storage in a computer. A byte contains eight binary digits. See *bit.*

Cache. A separate area of *RAM* that stores frequently used instructions or data so the *CPU* can use them more quickly than if they were stored on a disk or in another area of memory.

Capture. To store automatically on disk the data being transferred by a *terminal program* in *terminal mode.*

CD-ROM (Compact Disk-Read Only Memory) **drive.** A *disk drive* that reads prerecorded compact disks (CDs) containing computer information, video, or sounds.

Cell. One data storage location in a spreadsheet. A typical spreadsheet contains thousands of cells.

Cell address. The location of a particular spreadsheet *cell,* as indicated by the row and column number whose intersection the cell represents.

Cell reference. A *cell address* used in a spreadsheet *formula.*

Character. A single letter, number, or punctuation mark in a *document* or *file.*

Checkbox. A graphical box inside a *dialog box* that selects or deselects an option.

Chip. A tiny sandwich made of silicon and other materials that performs a certain function in a computer. Also called a semiconductor.

Circuit board. A piece of plastic containing *chips* and other electrical devices.

Clicking. Pressing the *mouse* or *trackball* button to *select* something or perform an action on the computer screen. See *Selecting*.

Client. A computer (or the person using the computer) that uses shared services on a computer *network*.

Client software. A *network communications* program that allows a computer to access shared services on a computer *network*.

Clipboard. A portion of the computer's *memory* that temporarily stores *selections* of *data* that you *cut* or *copy* from a *document*.

Clock/calendar chip. A *chip* in a computer that keeps track of the current time and date. A battery inside the computer maintains the correct time and date in this chip when the computer is shut off.

Close box. A small box in the upper left corner of a *window* that closes the window when you click it. See *Clicking, Window*.

Command. An instruction you give a computer.

Command key. A key on a computer *keyboard* whose only function is to issue commands when pressed at the same time as other keys.

Command line interface. A method of controlling a computer that requires you to remember and type commands.

Communications port. A plug on the back of a computer intended for connecting a *network* cable, *modem,* or other communications device.

Component. Any individual piece of computer equipment, such as a *monitor, system unit, keyboard,* or *printer.*

CONFIG.SYS file. A *file* that is loaded by the *operating system* when you turn on a *PC-compatible computer* and that adjusts the way the operating system uses *memory* and *files.*

Continuous paper. Paper for computer printers that is used in one continuous strip, with perforations to separate the pages.

Control panel. A *program* that modifies or helps you adjust the *operating system* software on a *Macintosh* computer.

Copying. Placing a duplicate of a *selection* of *data* from a *document* on the *clipboard* by *selecting* it and choosing the program's Copy command.

CPU (central processing unit). The *chip* that acts as the computer's brain, interpreting and carrying out instructions to process information. Also called a microprocessor or processor, as in Intel 80486 processor and PowerPC processor.

Crash. A software error that causes a *program* to become unusable and that usually forces the user to restart the computer.

Cursor. A blinking vertical line or box that shows where *data* will appear when you type. Also called an *insertion point.*

Cutting. Removing *data* from a *document* by *selecting* it and choosing the program's Cut command.

Data. The words, numbers, facts, sounds, or other information you store, manipulate, and transfer with a computer.

Data bits. A setting in a *terminal program* that determines the size of each chunk of *data* being transferred.

Data entry. 1. The act of typing or otherwise storing data in a *document*. 2. A piece of computer *data* stored in a database *field* or spreadsheet *cell*.

Data format settings. A group of settings in a *terminal program* that determines the size and other characteristics of data chunks being transferred.

Data type. An *attribute* of a database *field* that determines how information in that field is treated by the program.

Default. A factory or standard setting in a *program* or hardware *component*.

Default value. A predefined entry that automatically appears in a database *field*.

Define. To create a database *field*.

Desktop. The portion of a *graphical user interface* that displays *disks* and their contents.

Desktop computer. A computer made up of separate *components* designed to fit on or underneath a desk or table.

Dial-up connection. A communications link between two computers that is accomplished by placing a call on a telephone line.

Dialog box. A box that appears on the screen and that contains options you must choose or requests information you must supply in order to complete a command.

Directory (also called a *Folder*). A named area on a *disk* where a particular collection of *files* can be stored.

Disk. A storage device for computer *data* or *programs*.

Disk drive. A device that stores (writes) or retrieves (reads) information on magnetic *disks*.

Document. The contents of a *file* when the file is open and you are working with it on the screen, as in *word-processing document*.

Dot matrix printer. A computer *printer* that makes characters by pressing pins in different patterns against an inked ribbon.

Downloading. Copying or retrieving a *file* from another computer.

Dragging. Holding down the *mouse* or *trackball* button after selecting an item and then moving the *pointer* to move a *disk, folder, file icon,* or another *selection* from one place to another on the screen. See *Selecting.*

Drawing program. A program that allows you to create and manipulate shapes and lines.

Dual-mode key. A *keyboard* key that performs one of two functions, depending on the position of the [Num Lock] key.

Duplex. A setting in a communications program that determines whether *data* being sent in *terminal mode* is displayed on the sender's screen.

Edit. To change the contents of a *document*. Also a common name for a *menu* that offers editing commands in a *program*.

Electronic mail. A *network communications* program that allows users to send and receive messages.

Entry bar. A graphical box at the top of a spreadsheet's *document window,* which shows the contents of the selected *cell.*

Entry box. A graphical box inside a *dialog box* where you type information needed to complete a command.

Expansion board. A *circuit board* that plugs into a computer's *expansion slot.*

Expansion slot. A special connector inside the computer where you can plug in a *circuit board* to expand your computer's capabilities. See *Circuit board, Expansion board.*

Export. To save a *file* in a *format* that can be read by a different program from the one you're using. See *Format, 3.*

Extension. A type of *program* loaded when you start a *Macintosh* computer, which modifies the function of the *operating system.*

Fax modem. A communications device that allows a computer to exchange information with a fax machine via a telephone line.

Field. A category of information in a database file.

File. A collection of *data* or a *program* stored on a disk.

File server. A networked computer whose disks are available as storage for other network users.

File transfer method. A means of transferring certain types of files with a particular *file transfer protocol* in a *terminal program.*

File transfer protocol. A set of rules that handle the transfer of files in a *terminal program.*

Finding. See *Selecting, 2.*

First-line indent. An indent that applies only to the first line of a paragraph in a word-processing *document.*

Flat-file database. A database *program* that works with information in only one *file* at a time.

Floating point unit. A special *microprocessor* (or part of a microprocessor) that speeds mathematical calculations.

Floppy disk. A removable plastic *disk* on which computer *data* is stored.

Floppy disk drive. A disk drive that reads and writes *floppy disks.*

Folder. See *Directory.*

Font. A typeface.

Footer. *Data* that appears in the same position at the bottom of each page in a *document.*

Form. An arrangement of database *fields* on the screen for data entry.

Format. 1. (v) To prepare a *disk* so it can store *data* from a computer. 2. (n) A particular *disk* storage method, as in *IBM-format disk* or *Macintosh-format disk.* 3. (n) A particular *file* storage method, as in *WordPerfect format* or *Microsoft Word format.*

Formula. A set of calculating instructions stored in a spreadsheet *cell* or database *field.*

Forum. A discussion group on an *on-line computer service* where users can post and read messages on specific subjects.

Freeze. A software error in which the *program* no longer responds to *commands.*

Function. A predefined calculating instruction that is used in a *formula.*

Function key. A *keyboard* key that executes a specific *command* in a *program.* Function keys can perform different commands in different programs.

Gate. A switch inside a *microprocessor.* A typical microprocessor has more than a million gates.

Graphical user interface (GUI). A method of controlling a computer that allows you to *select* and *click* items or choose *commands* from *menus.*

Hard disk drive. A *disk drive* that uses an aluminum, nonremovable disk to store computer *data.*

Hardware. The physical *components* that make up a computer.

Hayes command set. A standard set of *commands* used by a *terminal program* to control a *modem.*

Header. Data that appears in the same position at the top of each page in a *document,* or the part of a database *report format* that contains header information.

IBM-compatible computer. A computer that runs the PC-DOS, MS-DOS, or OS/2 *operating system.*

Icon. A tiny picture that represents a *disk, directory, folder,* or *file* in a *graphical user interface.*

Import. To use a *program* to open a *file* created with a different program.

Indent controls. Graphical symbols that can be *dragged* in a word-processing document's *ruler* to change the amount by which a paragraph is indented from the right and left margins.

Init. See *Extension.*

Ink jet printer. A computer *printer* that makes characters by spraying ink onto paper in various patterns.

Input/Output (I/O) port. A plug where you connect a *monitor, keyboard, modem,* and other *components* to the *system unit.*

Insertion point. See *Cursor.*

Installed base. The total number of people using a particular computer, program, or other computer product.

Interface. The method by which you communicate with a personal computer. See *Command line interface, Graphical user interface.*

Internet. A worldwide network that links thousands of individual computer networks at universities, corporations, and government agencies, enabling the exchange of *data* and *electronic mail* among users of those networks.

Internet services provider. A company whose network is connected to the *Internet* and that provides outside users with access to the Internet for a fee.

Invisible character. A *character* in a word-processing *document* that can be displayed on the screen but does not appear on paper when the document is printed.

Item. A graphical object that can be opened, moved, or otherwise manipulated in a *graphical user interface.*

Justified text. Paragraphs in a word-processing *document* in which the words are evenly aligned on both the left and right margins.

Keyboard. A set of typewriter-like keys you use to control the computer or to type information into *documents.*

Keyboard shortcut. A sequence of keys you press to execute a *command,* rather than choosing the command from a *menu* with a *mouse.*

Kilobyte. 1,024 *bytes* of computer storage or *memory,* also known as *k,* as in "800k disk."

Laptop computer. A portable computer whose *components* all fit in a box about the size of a three-ring binder.

Laser printer. A computer *printer* that works by fusing powdered ink (toner) onto sheets of paper.

Layout. See *Form.*

Line length. A *terminal program* setting that determines the length of lines of *data* in the communications *document window.*

Load. To take instructions from a *disk* or other storage device and place them into *RAM*, as in *load a program* or *load a file.*

Local area network. A group of computers linked by a cable in an office.

Local echo. See *Duplex.*

Log on. To establish a connection with a *local area network* or *on-line computer service.*

Logic board. A large *circuit board* that holds the computer's main *chips* and handles its basic functions.

Lookup field. A *field* in one database *file* where entering *data* causes the program to find and retrieve information from a different database file.

Macro. A *command* that executes a series of other commands.

Macintosh. A personal computer sold by Apple Computer. Also called a Mac.

Macintosh System. The *operating system* that runs *Macintosh* computers.

Mail server. A computer on a *network* that manages the storage and transmission of *electronic mail* messages.

Main directory. See *Root directory.*

Megabyte. A million bytes of memory or storage (1,048,576, to be exact). Also known as MB, as in "100MB disk drive." See *byte.*

Megahertz (abbreviated as *MHz*). Millions of electrical cycles (hertz) per second. Computer *microprocessor* speeds are measured in megahertz.

Memory. A group of *chips* where the computer temporarily stores information. See *RAM*.

Memory-resident program. A program on a *PC* or *Macintosh* that adds extra functions to the *operating system* or to an *application program* and that runs without user intervention. See also *Extension*.

Menu. A named list of *commands* by which you control a *program* or *graphical user interface*. You display a menu by *selecting* the menu name, then choose a *command* by selecting its name from the menu.

Menu bar. An area at the top of the screen (or at the top of an open *window*) that contains the names of *menus*.

Microprocessor. A computer *chip* that executes instructions — the "brain" of a computer.

Microsoft Windows. A *graphical user interface* that is used with the *MS-DOS operating system*.

Model. A spreadsheet *document* that contains rows and columns of numbers, dates, times, labels, and formulas.

Modem. A *component* that connects your computer to a telephone line and allows it to communicate with other computers. The modem *mo*dulates and *dem*odulates sounds to translate them into computer data; hence the name.

Modem port. A setting in a *terminal program* that specifies which *communications port* the modem is connected to.

Modem settings. A group of settings in a *terminal program* that sets up the program to work properly with a particular type of modem and determines how that modem will be used.

Modem type. A setting in a *terminal program* that specifies the brand and model of modem being used.

Monitor. A video screen that shows what's going on as you work with the computer.

Mount. To establish a connection with a particular *disk* or *directory* on a *network file server* so you can use it to store or retrieve *files*.

Mouse. A small box that you roll around on your desktop to control a *pointer* on the computer screen.

Mouse button. A button on a *mouse* that you press, or *click,* to choose, or *select,* something on the computer screen.

MS-DOS. An operating system sold by Microsoft Corporation and used to run *PC-compatible* computers.

Multimedia. A catch-all term for computer systems that can store, record, and play back sounds, pictures, and video as well as printed information.

Native format. The unique file-recording method normally used by a particular program when a *document* is saved. For example, a file saved with WordPerfect would normally be saved in WordPerfect's *native format.*

Navigation keys. The keys on a *keyboard* that you use to move the *cursor* around in a *document* or *dialog box,* or to *scroll* a document *window.*

Network. A group of computers linked together.

Network administrator. A person responsible for maintaining a computer network.

Network communications. A means of communications in which a group of computers are linked via cables, telephone lines, or satellite transmissions so that they can exchange information easily.

Numeric keypad. A separate group of keys on a *keyboard* that produce numbers or move the *cursor* when you press them.

On-line computer service. A large computer that offers games, shopping, electronic mail, information, and other services to subscribers, who access it via *dial-up connections.*

Operating system. Software that prepares the *CPU* to receive further instructions from you and that you use to manage *disks,* run *programs,* and adjust the computer's hardware.

Orphan. One short line of a paragraph in a word-processing *document* that appears by itself at the bottom of a page.

OS/2. A relatively new personal computer *operating system* sold by IBM that includes a *graphical user interface.*

Page break. A *command* in a word-processing or spreadsheet *program* that forces the program to begin printing on a new page.

Page layout program. A *program* that lets you arrange words and graphics on a page to create brochures, newsletters, and other publication-quality materials.

Page view mode. See *Preview mode.*

Painting program. A *program* that allows you to create graphic images by manipulating individual points of light, or *pixels,* on a computer screen.

Paragraph marker. An *invisible character* that forces a word-processing *program* to begin a new paragraph on a new line.

Parity bits. A setting in a *terminal program* that determines whether or not the program checks for the accuracy of data transmissions in *terminal mode*.

Password. A secret word or code that you use to gain access to an *on-line computer service* or to a restricted portion of a database *file*.

Pasting. Taking the contents of a program's *clipboard* and placing them at the *cursor* position by choosing the Paste command from the program's Edit menu.

PC. Another name for *IBM-compatible computer*, after the original IBM Personal Computer, which was called the IBM PC for short.

PC-compatible computer. See *IBM-compatible computer*.

PC-DOS. IBM's version of the *operating system* that runs most IBM-compatible personal computers. See *MS-DOS*.

Pixel. One point of light on a computer screen. A typical screen contains thousands of pixels.

Pointer. The arrow, *cursor*, or other graphic item on your screen that moves when you move a *mouse* or *trackball* on your desk.

Pointing. Using a *mouse* or *trackball* to control a *pointer* on the computer screen.

Port. See *Input/Output*.

Preview mode. A display option in a *program* that shows how a *document* will appear with its page margins when printed.

Print server. A kind of *network communications* software that allows a computer to route *documents* sent from other network users to a *printer* elsewhere on the network.

Printer. A *component* that reproduces computer *files* or *documents* on paper.

Productivity program. A *program* you use to create *documents* that store information.

Program. Any piece of *software* that controls a computer or makes it do something specific.

Pulse dialing. An option in a *terminal program* that instructs a *modem* to mimic a rotary-dial telephone when dialing a number.

Query screen. An arrangement of empty *fields* in a database *file* in which you enter criteria to *find* or *select* a particular group of *records*.

RAM (random access memory). A *chip* or group of *chips* that provides temporary storage for the computer instructions or data needed by the *CPU*.

Range. A group of adjacent spreadsheet *cells*.

Record. One related group of facts in a database *file*, such as one address or one inventory listing.

Redial option. A setting in a *terminal program* that determines if, when, and how often a *modem* will redial a telephone number if the line is busy or the call isn't answered.

Reformat. To change the arrangement (but not the content) of words in a word-processing *document*.

Relational database. A database program that can manage *data* in more than one *file* at a time.

Relative cell reference. A *cell reference* in a spreadsheet *formula* that changes, depending on the location of the formula itself.

Remote communications. Computer communications that link just two computers.

Removable hard disk drive. A *disk drive* that stores information on removable aluminum *disks,* each of which can store from twenty to forty thousand pages of data.

Report. Information from a database that is printed on paper.

Report format. An arrangement of database *fields* that will be printed on paper.

Return character. See *Paragraph marker.*

ROM (read-only memory). A computer *chip* that has instructions permanently etched into it.

Root directory. The lowest level of organization on a *disk,* which shows all of the disk's available space and any *files, folders,* or other *directories* on it.

Ruler. A graphical area at the top of a word processor's *document window* that shows the width of each line typed and allows you to set indents, line spacing, and tabs.

Run. To activate a *program* so its instructions control the computer, as in "run a program."

Script. See *Macro.*

Scroll arrow. A graphical arrow at the end of a *scroll bar* that you can click to display the next page of a *document* inside a *window.*

Scroll bar. An area at the right or bottom of a *window* that you use to see another portion of the *document* inside the window.

Scroll box. A graphical box inside a *scroll bar* that you can *drag* to display another part of the *document* in a *window* quickly.

Scrolling. Using a *scroll bar* to view a different portion of a *document* in a *window.*

Section break. A command that divides a word-processing *document* into different areas, each of which can then accept different margins, page numbers, or other options that would normally affect whole pages or an entire document.

Selecting. 1. Choosing a *menu, command,* or another *item* on a computer screen by *pointing* to it. 2. Locating and displaying a group of *records* in a database *file* based on the contents of those records.

Selection. Whatever is currently selected on a computer screen. See *Selecting.*

Selection outline. A darkened rectangle that surrounds the selected *cell* in a spreadsheet.

Server. A computer on a *network* that makes its *disks* or other services available to other computers on the network.

Server software. A *program* that instructs a computer to make its *disks* or other services available to other computers on a *network.*

Size box. A small box in the lower right corner of a *window* that you *drag* to make the window larger or smaller on the screen. See *Dragging, Window.*

Software. Recorded instructions, or *programs,* that make a computer perform specific operations.

Sort. To arrange database *records* or spreadsheet rows or columns in alphabetical, numerical, or chronological order.

Sound board. An *expansion board* that improves a computer's sound-producing capabilities.

Speakers. A set of stereo speakers connected to a computer to improve its sound output quality.

Speed. A *terminal program* setting that determines the speed at which data is transferred. See *bps.*

Spelling checker. A feature of most word-processing *programs*, which examines a *document*, compares its words with those in a built-in dictionary, and reports discrepancies.

Spontaneous quit. A *software* error that causes a *program* to close itself without warning.

Standard value. See *Default value.*

Status bar. An area at the bottom of a *document window* that shows the current page number, cursor location, and other information about the document.

Stop bits. A *data format* setting in a *terminal program* that determines how many *bits* are used to separate one chunk of data from another during transmissions in *terminal mode.*

Storage. A permanent place where you can store computer *data* or *programs,* usually a *disk.*

Style. An option that affects the appearance of text or numbers on the screen without changing their *font* or font size, such as boldfacing, underlining, and italicizing. Also, a common name for a *menu* that contains *commands* for different styles.

Submodel. A group of filled spreadsheet rows and columns that is calculated separately from other filled rows and columns in the same *document.*

Subsystem. A *circuit board, logic board, video board,* or another group of *components* that is usually installed and replaced as a unit.

Surge protector. A special power adapter that protects a computer and its *components* from fluctuations in the AC power level.

System requirements. A list that details the kind of computer, *op-*

erating system version, and other specifics required by a particular *program* or component.

System unit. The main box in the computer system, which usually contains the computer *chips, circuit boards,* power supply, and *disk drives.* (Also sometimes erroneously called the *CPU.*)

Terminal mode. The method of operating a *terminal program* that allows you to exchange *data* and *commands* with the remote computer by typing or *pasting data* in a *document window.*

Terminal program. A *program* that allows your computer to make and manage a connection with one other computer at a time over telephone lines or a cable.

Terminal settings. A group of options in a *terminal program* that controls the appearance of *data* on the screen in *terminal mode.*

Text format. See *ASCII format.*

Title bar. An area at the top of a *window* that contains the window's name and *close box.*

Tone dialing. An option in a *terminal program* that instructs a *modem* to dial a call using the same tones generated by a push-button phone.

Tool bar. A group of frequently used *menus* or *buttons* that appear below the *menu bar* in some programs.

Trackball. An upside-down *mouse* in which you roll a ball set into a stationary box to move the *pointer* on the screen.

TSR. A *memory-resident program* on a PC-compatible computer.

Type-ahead buffer. A portion of the computer's *memory* that captures and stores keystrokes when the computer is too busy to respond to them immediately.

Typewriter-like keys. The main group of keys on a computer *keyboard*, which resembles the set of keys on a typewriter.

UPS (uninterruptible power supply). A battery that supplies power to a computer during an AC power failure.

User name. The name by which someone is identified on a computer *network* or *on-line computer service*.

Utility program. An *application program* that makes the computer perform a very specific task, usually a housekeeping task such as repairing a damaged disk or checking the computer system for *viruses*.

Video board. A *circuit board* that generates the video signal that displays the computer's activity on a *monitor*.

Virus. A *program* that performs destructive or annoying actions on a computer, such as erasing or renaming *files* at random, and that copies itself from one *disk* to another.

Wide area network. A group of *local area networks* within one company or organization that are all connected via telephone lines, fiber optic cabling, or satellite or microwave links.

Widow. The short last line of a paragraph in a word-processing *document* when it appears by itself at the top of a page.

Window. A graphical box on the screen that displays a *document*.

Windows PC. A *PC-compatible* computer that is running the Microsoft Windows *graphical user interface*.

Word wrap. A feature in word-processing *programs* that automatically places text on a new line when the line you're typing on fills up.

Index

trackball, 90, 244, 265
troubleshooting, 227–232, 247–253
TSRs, 113
turbo button, 86
type-ahead buffer, 121

Undo command, 246
unexpected results, 243
uninterruptible power supply, 120–121
used computers, 36–39
user groups, 50, 256
user name, 216
utility programs, 57, 113

VGA, 44
video board, 2
video memory, 44
video output, 44–46
viruses, 116–118, 249
vision problems, 83

warranty cards, 78
White House, 223
wide area network, 210

window, 12, 13, 16–19
Windows. *See* Microsoft Windows
word-processing computer, 27
word-processing program, 56, 123–132
  bold type, 136
  changing font or style, 131–132, 136
  character formatting, 136–137, 145
  checking spelling, 131
  copying text, 130
  cursor, 88–89, 124–125, 128
  cutting and pasting text, 130
  difference from typewriter, 139–142
  document formatting, 138–139
  entering/editing text, 127–131
  extra paragraphs or spaces, 141
  first-line indents, 124–125, 141–142
  format overload, 144–146
  formatting options, 131–132, 135–139
  garbage characters, 149–150